Arranging Techniques for Synthesists.

by Eric Turkel.

Arranging Techniques for Synthesists.

by Eric Turkel.

&

Amsco Publications.
London/New York/Sydney

Edited by Elizabeth Smith-Eisenhower
Illustrations by L. Vogler

Copyright © 1988 by Amsco Publications,
A Division of Music Sales Corporation, New York, NY.

International Standard Book Number: 0.8256.1130.X

Exclusive Distributors:
Music Sales Corporation
24 East 22nd Street, New York, NY 10010 USA
Music Sales Limited
8/9 Frith Street, London W1V 5TZ England
Music Sales Pty. Limited
120 Rothschild Street, Rosebery, Sydney, NSW 2018, Australia

Printed in the United States of America by
Vicks Lithograph and Printing Corporation

ACKNOWLEDGMENTS

Special thanks to Holly Gewandter, Howard Massey, Peter Pickow, Dan Earley, Amy Appleby, everyone at Amsco Publications, my wife Maureen, my family, Joe Cain, Peter Darmi, Ken Hitchcock, Dave Lavender, Palomba Music, Stan Polanski, Mike Selverne, Alec Shantzis, Jimmy Vallis, Alan Zahn, Tony Zano, and dozens of great teachers and friends for their endless sense of humor, support, and inspiration.

Lack of opportunity is usually nothing more than a lack of purpose or direction.   Anonymous

CONTENTS

INTRODUCTION

This book is designed for the amateur or professional musician who wants to increase his or her knowledge of arranging. Even though it focuses on techniques for the electronically oriented musician, an understanding of acoustic instruments and voices will improve any musician's knowledge of sound production and arranging skills.

A few MIDI keyboards, a sequencer, and a drum machine are enough tools to explore the techniques outlined in this book. If you play any acoustic instruments, or have access to any obliging singers, then you can experiment with combinations of electronic and acoustic sounds.

No matter what your involvement in music is, a solid knowledge of arranging will make your contribution more valuable. Practically speaking, the ability to function as an arranger affords you more control over the recording and performance of your music.

This book examines the basic tools used in developing an arrangement. By first understanding the limitations of a situation, you can develop the techniques to stretch creativity beyond those limits.

The book does not attempt to define what styles of music are good or bad. That issue is totally subjective—a matter of personal taste. By attempting to master the skills of arranging, however, we musicians can improve the music we find good.

Also, a few thoughts on the word *commercial*. This word often implies some sort of value judgment. Commercial music is music that sells. It sells to people who have decided that it adds some value to their lives. There is good and bad commercial music, just as there is good and bad music that claims to be purely artistic. It's up to you to make the intellectual and emotional decisions about the music with which you become involved.

We have all been told that "practice makes perfect," which is a myth worth exploring. Although the statement is usually well intentioned, the fact is that only "perfect practice makes perfect!" To put it simply: if you spend weeks or years practicing the wrong way, you end up perfecting a bad habit and wasting valuable time. Practicing "hard" has little value in and of itself unless you also practice "smart." This means that your effort is yielding the intended result and that you understand why you are doing what you are doing. There has to be a reason and a goal for practicing and developing technique.

What is technique, anyway? Generally speaking, technique is the ability to communicate ideas effectively to as many people as possible. Technique is not something acquired or hoarded for its own sake, rather it is a means to a musical end. The best techniques are those that give results and communicate effectively. It is one thing to imitate "hip" chord voicings and another to understand the concept behind those voicings. Understanding the concept gives you a powerful tool and reasons to use it.

It is also important to remember that at the foundation of a strong arrangement lie several well-developed ideas. You shouldn't try to cram everything you know into one four-minute piece of music. Choose the important ideas and develop them thoroughly over the course of an arrangement. A piece of music with too many good ideas lacks focus, and a piece of music (no matter how well arranged) with undeveloped or trite ideas will lack impact. These are the two extremes to avoid. You need inspiration and the technique to communicate it effectively.

The arranger initially views a piece of music as a skeleton—hopefully, a solid, strong one—which is to be filled out with musical parts that fulfill the various needs of the project. For example, if someone asks you to arrange an R&B dance song, that request has specific directions about style, tempo, instrumentation, length, and so forth. You have now been directed to a specific area and set of guidelines with which to work. Yet within these restrictions there is plenty of room for creativity. There are many interesting rhythmic, melodic, harmonic, form, and dynamic twists and turns to take. The only real limits inside this "ball park" are your imagination and the technique you have to execute ideas. This is what makes one arrangement brilliant and another in the same style ordinary or dull. Powerful imagination coupled with strong technique allows you to develop arrangements that have impact and that are memorable.

By working within certain limitations, you can be more creative because you are focused and the infinite choices are narrowed down to the appropriate. In pop arranging, the style of a project is often the most important guide to making arranging decisions. The more familiar you are with different styles, the more valuable you are as an arranger.

The art and craft of arranging has taken on new dimensions in the last several years, largely due to MIDI. There now is an infinite (and affordable) choice of sounds and textures available from MIDI synths and samplers. When these are coupled with sequencers, computers, modern recording, and signal processing, there are possibilities and control that were beyond our wildest dreams only a few years ago.

While technology has changed rapidly, the principles of arranging remain unchanged. Arranging is still the art and craft of creating and organizing musical parts to support a given work. Technology is a powerful tool, not a replacement for solid musical thought. It gives us control over our music in ways never before available, but the music still should have substance on its own. Technology can challenge, stimulate, and give us ways of hearing and manipulating music we may never have considered. We can play fascinating games with musical ideas, but the music still sounds best when it is strong from the start. Giving someone a word processor won't automatically make him or her a Shakespeare. Don't let your musical development be stunted or overshadowed by a fascination with technology. As amazing and powerful as it is, it's still a tool.

Our responsibilities as arrangers are not unlike those of gourmet chefs. We have to assemble many ingredients into an exciting, satisfying, and aesthetically pleasing package. We need a good amount of inspiration and technique to be effective. There are only so many chords, drum beats, and notes, yet it's how they are assembled that makes a work sound fresh and memorable. The elements of music—rhythm, harmony, melody, form, timbre, and idiom (style)—are the arranger's tools, or ingredients.

This book examines the planning and development of an arrangement. It also discusses the issues, problems, and solutions in various arranging situations.

MIDI allows us to experiment freely and develop in ways that would have been impossible a few years ago. There is a way of realizing ideas and developing techniques that were once the exclusive property of a select few. The substance of arranging involves being capable of developing, organizing, controlling, and executing musical ideas. Hopefully, *you* have the creative urge and inspiration. This book will supply you with the techniques to realize your goals.

CHAPTER ONE
UNDERSTANDING FORM

Form is one of the more difficult of the six musical elements to define or describe. We don't "hear" form; we feel it. We are least aware of form when an arrangement flows from introduction to ending in an exciting, engaging way. We occasionally become aware of it when sections don't flow together and end up with a sense that something is missing or not connecting. Form is like a blueprint from which we develop a solid structure. Weak form leaves us with a feeling of incompletion caused by a flaw in the blueprint, which inevitably leads to structural damage.

Form is the division of space or time into units or distinct sections. We set these divisions up at specific lengths for technical and aesthetic reasons. Form is the silent yet pervasive force that holds an arrangement together.

Musical form closely resembles the development of human life, and thus there are many obvious comparisons to the life cycle. In western music form is invariably at the core of composition. Here is the basic form we will use for comparison: Introduction, theme and variations, development, recapitulation (repeat of themes), and coda. Let's look at each section individually.

1. **Introduction.** Material that is directly related to, or derived from, the body of the work. *Comparison:* spring—the time when growth begins; birth—the introduction of a new person related to and derived from its parents.

2. **Theme and Development.** The exposure and development of the body of the form—verses and choruses that contain the message(s) of the music. The majority of the arrangement is developed and explored in these sections, which often include solo passages. *Comparison:* summer—traditionally the time of growth and development. This musical area parallels physical, spiritual, and mental development. Goals and purposes become clear and realized. Major achievements and contributions occur (solos). The messages contained in choruses and verses are developed. Verses can be thought of as information that supports and builds toward the primary statement, the chorus. Verses can be thought of as evidence, and choruses as conclusions or verdicts.

3. **Recapitulation.** The primary themes are stated again, often in a different setting. This is also where the *bridge* (transition) section occurs. The bridge allows us to view the preceding music in a different way; it offers some perspective before the ending. By now the message has been delivered; it is mature. *Comparison:* this section is like fall, the harvest season. We have planted and developed the seeds, now we harvest the crop. This is the transition section where we move toward the end of the musical-life cycle. The bridge, or fall, offers a pause for reflection before moving toward the ending.

4. **Coda.** Finale. The themes draw to their logical conclusion. In a pop arrangement, the ending is usually a chorus section (the big message), either with a written or fade ending. This is the final statement, which often highlights the main themes. *Comparison:* winter (end, death, rest). It is not uncommon to reflect back on the highlights and main themes of one's life during winter. This is sometimes relived through a second childhood or senility. The end comes in many ways—quickly, peacefully, abruptly, or slowly. The music ends quickly or can fade gradually.

Planning an Arrangement

Arrangements usually contain three main sections—verse, chorus, and bridge. Introductions and interludes are subsections between the main sections. For purposes of illustration, we will use the following standard abbreviations:

I	=	Introduction
Int	=	Interlude
A	=	Verse
B	=	Chorus
C	=	Bridge

Here are three of the most effective and widely used forms in modern arranging.

1. I A B A C A B

2. I A B A B C A B (In this version the second chorus precedes the bridge.)

3. I A B A B B C A B (In this version a double chorus precedes the bridge.)

Only the order of sections is indicated, not the particular instruments or orchestration within the sections. Here are three quick definitions that should help keep things clear.

1. *Form* The order of sections.

2. *Arrangement* The rhythmic, harmonic, melodic, and stylistic direction given to specific instruments.

3. *Orchestration* Assigning sounds to notes.

Most pop arrangements are between 3 and 4 minutes long and average 80 to 144 beats per minute (bpm). To see how this 3- to 4-minute arrangement evolved, we will use the following form and tempo as an example: I A B A C A B, a quarter note = 120 bpm, $\frac{4}{4}$ time.

Let's assume that the verses are 16 bars long, as are the choruses and the bridge. Three 16-bar verses will therefore equal a total of 48 measures; two 16-bar choruses will equal a total of 32 measures; one 16-bar bridge will equal a total of 16 measures. The entire form adds up to 96 measures of music.

Ninety-six measures of music at 4 beats per measure ($\frac{4}{4}$) gives us a total of 384 beats. Dividing the total number of beats (384) by the tempo (120 bpm) gives us 3.2 minutes. If we add on an 8-measure introduction and two 4-bar interludes plus a fade ending, the arrangement totals 3.5 minutes. So, with a little basic math, we can see that it takes between 3 and 4 minutes to play through the form.

Tempo and the specific form will determine the exact timing, but exact timing isn't the point here; understanding the form is. Writing a 3- to 4-minute arrangement is the direct result of using form effectively. The primary message of an arrangement (found in the chorus) is delivered three times—at least twice in the body of the form and again at the end. Behavioral psychologists, market researchers, and sales experts tell us that a message has maximum impact with three repeats. Radio and television commercials certainly follow this rule.

The bridge section usually comes after the second verse, somewhere after the halfway point in an arrangement. If you look at how the form is constructed, you will see that there are two verses and at least one chorus before the bridge and usually one verse and chorus after the bridge. The bridge serves as a pause between two halves of a song. In effect we hear the song twice.

Verses/chorus(es) ——— Bridge ——— Verse/chorus
       (1)   (2)

Verse sections usually contain material that is in direct support of the chorus. Generally speaking, the verses contain the supporting "evidence" and the chorus is the "conclusion" (verdict).

There are two types of endings. Live or performance endings have a specific cutoff point, even if it is at the end of a vamp. Recorded endings either end specifically or fade out. In fact, recordings often have different endings for different mixes. A live or recorded ending will occasionally be abrupt or unpredictable. This can be a dramatic and powerful tool. Just when we expect a predictable part or cliché, our attention is redirected; and just like any strong seasoning or spice, a little bit goes a long way.

A beat or two of silence often appears between sections of the form, usually as a false ending to be followed by the same or new material. Fade endings serve to ease the listener gently out of the music and to release tension.

Regardless of the specific form used for a given project, the overall curve appears below. The climax point for an arrangement occurs approximately two-thirds to three-quarters to four-fifths of the way through the arrangement.

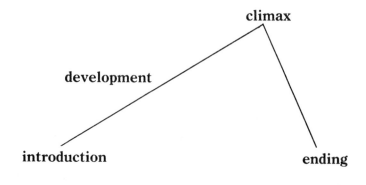

Table 1.1 illustrates how this curve develops. It is a general outline, not a rigid formula.

Table 1.1

Development of a Form's Overall Curve.

Simplicity	Complexity	Peak (Climax)	Return to Simplicity	Ending
Introduction, verse 1	Scoring (parts) becomes thicker, with more counterlines. Rhythmic activity increases. Texture becomes more dense.	Thickest, most complex area of arrangement.	Return to more transparent writing and playing with less activity and density.	Contains a fade or written ending usually based on the chorus section.
Light scoring	More dynamic contrast and intensity.	Loudest dynamics, or sharpest contrast of dynamics.	Dynamics decrease.	Intensity often peaks again, but not for very long.
Dynamics are soft relative to the ultimate goal. There should be room left to grow dynamically.	Increased harmonic tension to support melody or background. Richer vocal harmonies and voicings.	Maximum of harmonic tension in any and all parts.	Harmonic tension releases.	Arrangement gradually or abruptly ends.
Minimum of harmonic tension.	Instruments and voices move toward extremes. They are no longer restricted to midregister.	Use of extreme registers in instruments and voices.	Instruments and voices return to midregister.	
Instruments and voices are in midregister, with no extremes yet.	There are more rhythmic variations on melody, including ad-libs and harmonic, rhythmic, and melodic embellishments of melody.	High point of melodic range, with the most variations on melody present. Can include a solo (vocal or instrumental).	The melody is restated in its original version (rhythmically and melodically, if not lyrically).	
The melody is stated in its most basic way. There are no syncopations or embellishments yet.		Modulation(s) may occur.		

INTRODUCTIONS

It is wise not to write the introduction until you have written or developed ideas for your arrangement, simply because introductory material is usually derived from something in the body of the work. A melody, rhythm, counterline, sound, or texture that you develop in the arrangement will probably be a strong contender for the introduction (intro), so wait until things take shape before deciding on the material to use. Store your ideas in a sequencer. Here are some suggestions for sources of intro material.

1. The song will contain melodic fragments. Try using a fragment of the melody over different chord changes.

2. Use the chord changes from a verse or chorus or a variation on those chords.

3. Use material that is unrelated but that is in the same style of the project. Totally unrelated material sometimes is very effective in creating an element of surprise. Madonna's "Papa Don't Preach" begins with a classical-sounding string section only somewhat harmonically related to the body of the arrangement.

4. Use rhythmic patterns (*groove*) from the verse or chorus sections. This is a common way of setting up the groove in a pop arrangement.

5. If singers have to enter after the intro, make the transition harmonically and melodically comfortable. It is not necessary to have an instrument double the vocal lead-in notes; just don't take the intro to a harmonically obscure place and leave it without leading the singer in. This may work for an instrumental arrangement, but most singers are not comfortable with this approach. The chords can be subtle, but vocalists must be able to make strong, confident entrances.

6. You will occasionally write an intro based on a section or fragment of the arrangement, but write it in a different key. Having an intro in one key and then modulating it into the top of the arrangement can be very effective. Be careful to lead the vocalist into the modulation and through it to the top of the first verse.

MODULATIONS

Modulation is leaving one key and establishing another. There are two basic types of modulation—prepared and direct. A *prepared* modulation means you approach the new key via its V chord or substitute V chord. *Direct* modulation occurs when you leave one key and go directly to the next without establishing the new key via its V or substitute V7 chord. In general, it makes sense to determine the key to which you want to modulate and then work backwards to find a suitable chord progression. This can be compared to finding the point of departure (old key) and the destination (new key) and then filling in the blanks. Use a sequencer to try various modulations. Put each one on a separate track, and compare them. (See Examples 1.1 and 1.2.)

Prepared Modulations

Example 1.1

Example 1.1 *(continued)*

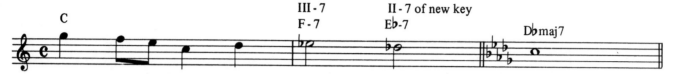

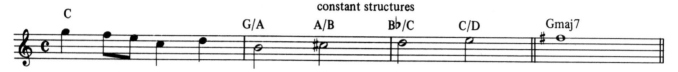

Example 1.1 *(continued)*

Direct Modulations

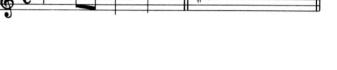

Example 1.2

Here are some common modulations. The chart is in the key of C but make an effort to learn these modulations in all twelve keys. They can be prepared or direct. Try both ways.

1.	up a minor second	C to D-flat
2.	up a major second	C to D
3.	up a minor third	C to E-flat
4.	up a major third	C to E
5.	up a perfect fourth	C to F*
6.	up an augmented fourth	C to F-sharp
7.	up a perfect fifth	C to G*
8.	up a minor sixth, or down a major third	C to A-flat

*These keys are so closely related that they are really not modulations, even though they can be effective.

9.	up a major sixth, or down a minor third	C to A
10.	up a minor seventh, or down a major second	C to B-flat
11.	Down a minor second	C to B

When you modulate to closely related keys, it's often more exciting to modulate into a distant key first and then work back to the closely related key. (This is similar to a quick double modulation.) Modulation does not imply going to a higher key; it just means going to another, or unrelated, key.

Using common tones is one of the most effective ways to modulate. Keeping a note common throughout the modulation into the new key is dramatic and builds continuity. It gives the listener a reference point through the transition. (See Example 1.3.)

Common-Tone Modulations

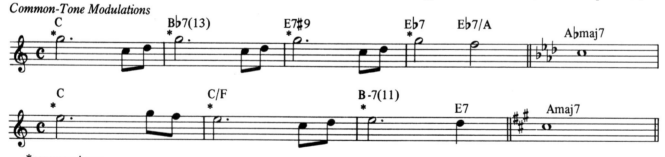

*common tones

Example 1.3

Material from your intro may appear in the modulation(s). Learn to modulate in the ways previously described by practicing the various techniques in all keys. Use melodic fragments from your verses or choruses to make the transition.

ENDINGS

An *ending* can be a simple repetition of the chorus, with a written or fade ending, or may be more involved. Here are some techniques for writing endings.

1. The ending may start out like a repetition of the chorus, but then develop with chord substitutions derived from or implied by the chorus's harmony. (See Example 1.4.)

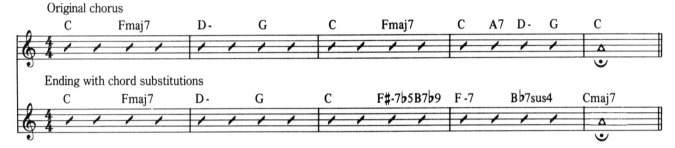

Example 1.4

2. The ending may use a deceptive cadence on the last note and may or may not resolve to the expected last chord. (See Example 1.5.)

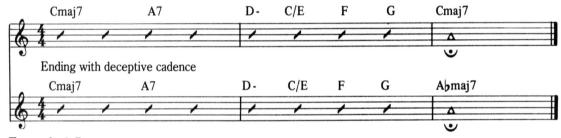

Example 1.5

3. The deceptive cadence can lead back into another repeat of the out-chorus or vamp. (See Example 1.6.)

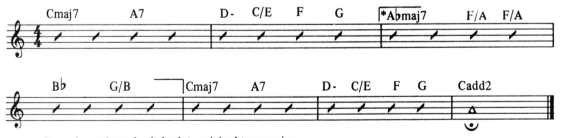

Deceptive cadence leads back to original progression.

Example 1.6

4. Drop one layer or instrument out at a time. For example, every four or eight bars you can delete an instrument or section until only one voice remains at the end. A variation on this involves dropping layers out and then building them back up to the final ending.

Introductions, modulations, and endings are great areas for special effects that might not be appropriate in the main body of the arrangement. Although most pop music is groove oriented, it is important to feature the subtle aspects of harmony, voicings, colors, and shading. Experiment by leaving out some of the basic rhythm-section elements so that the more subtle or transparent elements can stand out. The clever ideas you develop should appear at least two or three times throughout to build continuity. Try writing any number of alternate endings for your arrangements, based on these techniques. A sequencer can help you sort out the parts and the orchestration.

The following is an exercise which will help you organize and plan your arrangements. In order to become familiar with this routine, try applying to existing arrangements on record or tape. This is a two part exercise.

Part 1.

Lay out the sections of the arrangement on a plain piece of paper. Write the title, artist or group, and tempo at the top. This lets you see the form in a "naked" way.

Title

Artist   ♩ = 120

I   **A¹**   **A²**   **C**   **A³**   **B**   **B**   **fade**
                                                          |
                                                     guitar solo   modulation   fade

Note:

I = Intro

A¹ = verse 1, **A²** = verse 2, **A³** = verse 3 (in this case, a solo)

B = chorus, **B¹** = chorus in new key

　　　 = repeat and fade

fade

Part 2.

Using a separate sheet of paper for each section, describe in musical (or other) terms what is happening in that section. You will have as many sheets as there are sections. There are many synth sounds that have no standard names, so use your own descriptive terms. Here's an example of a page describing an introduction.

Example of Intro

1. Kick drum on beats 1 and 3. Snare drum on beat 4 of every second measure.

2. Hi hat and shaker (cabasa) play an eighth-note pattern with interesting accents. (Transcribe this!)

3. Bass line (sounds like an analog and digital combination) plays unaccented eighth notes.

4. There is a sustained keyboard pad (really fat and warm) in the middle register.

5. Two guitar parts. Part 1 is clean with chorus and delay. The playing is muted with a broken eighth-note pattern. Part 2 is a power chord. Sustain the part by playing whole notes along the chord progression.

6. Two chord vamp. Sounds like the I to IV chords with added seconds and no thirds. Each chord is held for four beats.

It's easy to see how much detail you can get into. Doing this exercise will improve your listening skills and become food for thought in your own work. You will learn about planning "musical menus" while analyzing the works of other arrangers.

Here is another useful checklist to go through when you begin to analyze a recording or to write your own arrangement. If this seems tedious and academic, realize that you are training your mind just as an athlete trains the body. There are no shortcuts—"no pain, no gain." All this will soon become instinctive. You need to program your mind with solid, high-yield techniques. Don't give up. It's worth it. Before you begin arranging a piece of music, do the following:

1. Become familiar with the melodic and harmonic content and any prominent rhythmic groove parts. Take notes, jot down the important information, or put it into a sequencer.

2. Read the lyrics (if any) and make a sincere effort to understand the mood or atmosphere of the piece. If you are working with a singer, try to find out what moves him or her (if anything) in the song. Don't worry. This is not a diversion into the depths of the singer's psyche, but you don't want to write generic arrangements.

3. Compile a list of important sounds, ideas, rhythms, melodies, harmonies, samples, and patches that may have value. See if you can list

your sounds according to the sections of the arrangement.

4. Write, sequence, and play some basic parts and drum patterns. Relate the sound to a part! If you are working on a keyboard pad part, don't use a horn-stab sample, or vice versa.

5. Try a few ideas for each section of the song. Vary the tempo and change some of the accents, syncopations, anticipations, or chord voicings. Shake it up a little bit. Don't just go with your first idea. It may be a great idea (and ultimately, the best one), but it will still be great an hour from now, so experiment! You can always return to it. Be sure to write the idea down or put it in your sequencer (and remember where). Lots of great ideas vanish when you trust only your memory. Back up your memory with the ancient art of writing on music paper or quickly put it in a trusty sequencer or computer. Exploring new territory often yields exciting and unexpected ideas. The worst thing that can happen by experimenting is that you will reconfirm what you already knew and return to your first idea.

6. Arranging is like assembling a jigsaw puzzle with more than one solution and too many pieces. Throw out (or save for another project) all but the best ideas. You decide which are best ideas by the fact that they are most consistent with the goals of the project. Keep an idea file or notebook. This is where disc-based sequencers are a blessing because for a few dollars, you can save thousands of useful fragments for future use or inspiration.

7. Work on the chorus section first. This is the most important and most remembered section. All your other ideas should lead to and away from it. Thus it makes sense to develop this section first. You have then got a reference point from which to work.

8. Write the verse sections after the chorus ideas are in place. Also, write your intro ideas after you have developed ideas for the choruses and verses. This allows you time to get to know this piece that's taking shape. It is very difficult to give a meaningful introduction to something you don't know yet.

9. Once you have made some firm decisions about the layout and content, record-sequence them and listen back. Do they work? Does what you are hearing sound like the ideas in your head? Is it better or worse?

10. Listen to the elements of the arrangement in isolation as well as with the whole. Do the sections flow well? Is there enough contrast? Check the rhythmic aspects of all the parts. Are there anticipations or syncopations that conflict and create unnecessary tension? This is a common problem, so check all the parts. These things often show up at unpleasant times, such as when you are working on vocals and all the keyboard pad parts are on a critical downbeat and the power

guitars are anticipating, when they really should coincide with everything else. Make sure all your parts work well together rhythmically.

11. Interludes are breathing space between sections. For example, a strong vocal or horn line sounds even better when it's not present 100 percent of the time. Listeners need to breathe as much as performers. The five senses need a rest to absorb what is happening. We all need brief pauses to reflect and assimilate before the next section.

12. Try to appeal to all five senses when you write. Behavioral psychologists claim that you will communicate best and have the greatest impact when your message engages all five senses. This is how your music becomes memorable and exciting. You can reach people on many levels by stimulating the senses. This is a key element of successful commercial arranging. Think of how that guitar part or horn break makes you feel. You know the feeling of elation when you hear a part of your own or on a record that instantly grabs your attention. That's not an intellectual response but an emotional one.

Overwriting and Keeping Perspective

The common problem of overwriting is often a result of playing or writing with an instrument that is not dependent on breath. All music must breathe. Even those relentless sequenced parts will drop out to leave some breathing space. Parts that don't breathe tend to make the listener uncomfortable and eventually bored.

Overwriting often happens when you work alone —playing, writing, and sequencing all the parts. You can become so obsessed with a part that you fail to realize it may actually be two or three parts meant for different timbres or instruments. Ask yourself what part(s) you are playing. Is it one part or more? An overactive left hand can also confuse things on keyboards. Try to simplify and separate your parts. Here is a final checklist of questions for your arrangement:

1. Is there a balance between repetition and variety of ideas?

2. Have you used a few ideas and developed them well?

3. Does the form work effectively? Is it supporting the music?

4. Does the arrangement climax at a logical place, around the two-thirds point?

5. Is the chord progression consistent and logical? Are there some refreshing harmonic alterations or surprises?

6. Is your choice of orchestration clear?

7. Do all the parts sound and feel good at the actual tempo? (When we work on sections in isolation, we sometimes forget about the ultimate tempo. We tend to work on difficult things at slower tempos.)

8. Are the parts consistent with the style of the music?

9. If individual parts are to be copied and read, are they copied neatly, accurately, and logically (with not too many shortcuts)? Are they transposed correctly? Are the dynamics properly placed? Are there phrasing and articulation markings, breath marks, and any special instructions?

10. If possible, sing through the parts (even if you don't have a great voice). Do the parts make sense by themselves, even if they are sweeteners or fills?

11. Do the sections have smooth transitions? Is there sufficient overlap in the orchestration to make smooth transitions?

12. Are the voicings balanced? Are there big gaps in any registers?

13. Are the parts balanced dynamically? Can you hear everything without straining? Is there an overall sense of depth and perspective? Does each part have its own place dynamically?

CHAPTER TWO ✍
MELODY

Before looking at the technical aspects of melody, it is useful to have an overview of what makes melody aesthetically pleasing. We listen to music on two levels—the mood or emotional level and the musical or technical level. There are certain universal characteristics of a well-developed melody, just as there are principles of coherence in form. Strong melody imparts a feeling of completion and wholeness. It is a challenge to create this mood and to make a definitive statement with a minimum of notes. This is not to say that strong melodies always have few notes. Rather, it means that the point is made in a graceful, concise, and focused way.

The vast majority of people who listen to music have no musical training. As creators, we have to satisfy both our musicianship and the average listener's needs. No small task! It is major achievement to satisfy your own artistic needs and still reach a wide audience. Stevie Wonder is a master at reaching almost everyone. His music has that universal ability to reach all ages and ethnic groups (including sophisticated musicians). Table 2.1 examines some of the universal qualities of a strong melody. The left side of the table lists some of the most common emotional responses to melody. The right side lists some of the technical-musical components that contribute to and evoke these emotional response.

There are two types of melody—written melody and improvised melody. *Written melody* is performed or recorded with only slight variations to the original. The melody can be subject to various interpretations but remains virtually the same. *Improvised melody* is developed or created spontaneously. It may (or may not) be based on a harmonic format. This type of melody has a "once-only" nature, although many improvised melodies (solos) are transcribed and reused later. In a sense, the composition of all melodies originates with improvisation.

TABLE 2.1.

Universal Qualities of a Strong Melody.

Mood-Senses	Technical-Musical
fulfillment	balance
wholeness	contrast
touch	repetition
taste	suggestion
smell	phrase structure
sight	symmetry, proportion
sound	articulation
anger	dynamics
love	anticipation
jealousy	delayed attacks
hope	syncopation
despair	accents
humor	interpretation
confidence	embellishment
sorrow	range
passion	chromaticism
	predictability
	surprise

Developing Interesting Melodies

The following is a list of questions and suggestions that will serve as a guide to developing melodies when they seem too predictable.

1. Does the melody stand alone? In other words, does it have a strong identity? Especially in the case of keyboard players, the melody becomes an afterthought to the chord changes or is so tied to the harmony that it can't survive alone. The next two suggestions should help solve this problem.

2. Try playing with one hand only. Don't play the chords; just play one note at a time, or even play with one or two fingers. This forces you to separate the melody from the related harmonic

framework. It is so tempting (especially with lots of "chops" and all the great sounds in our keyboards) to wander around the harmony and sounds, never really focusing on pure melody.

3. Try composing your melodies away from any instrument. Here's where ear training really helps. Can you hear or sing the melody? Never mind whether or not you have got a good voice; that's not the point. This is a great way to improve your interval recognition skills and try out your melodies. Use the keyboard (or any instrument) to verify what you are hearing after you have worked on it.

4. Does the melody have lack of direction, or is it too predictable? Is there too much repetition or not enough? The one extreme has many clichés; the other has incoherence (too many directions at once).

5. If your melodies seem too predictable or you just want some alternatives, try any or all of the techniques listed below. Most clichés started out as fresh ideas that eventually got overused. Understanding the concept behind the cliché helps us find variations or new uses for them. Let your ears be the final judge as to how useful they are in a given situation. If the results are not musical, singable, or somehow appropriate, modify or abandon them for another approach. A working knowledge of these techniques allows you to create many options and variations based on a single motif or melody. After working with these techniques, you will rarely get stuck for ideas. Any or all of the techniques presented in Examples 2.1 through 2.5 can be combined.

Original melody

Expanded range (varying intervals)

Contracted range (varying intervals)

Random changes of several intervals

Rhythmic shift of starting place

Addition of chromatic passing tones

Example 2.1

Original melody

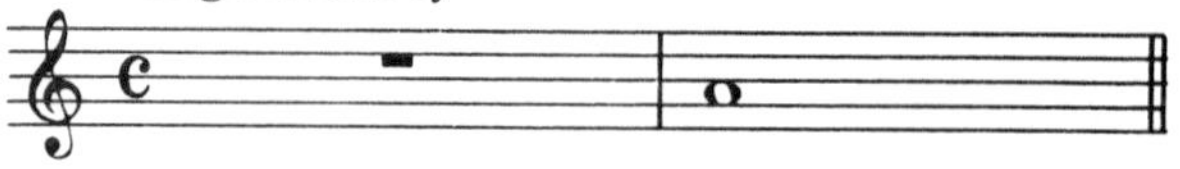

Anticipation    or   or

Delayed attack   or

Example 2.2

Original melody

Syncopation

Different time signature

Adding rests

Removing rests

Example 2.3

Original melody

Adding pickup notes and grace notes

Adding quarter-note triplets

Adding eighth-note triplets

Combining quarter-note and eighth-note triplets

Adding extra motifs derived from the melody

added motif   *added motif*

Example 2.4

Random augmentation and diminution

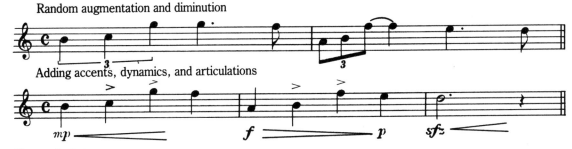

Adding accents, dynamics, and articulations

Example 2.5

Use a sequencer and try to keep the same melody and change the orchestration or sounds. Treat the melody contrapuntally. Switch between related major and minor keys. Orchestrate the same theme in different moods, or styles, using the same melody with new chords or even changing the order of notes in the melody. Don't panic! You can't do all of this in one day. Be patient. It gets easier in a short amount of time. Keep at it!

Developing Focused Melodies

The following is a list of suggestions for writing melodies that are focused with direction and unity and that don't contain too many elements and ideas.

1. Increase the repetition of the basic motifs (see "Repetition" below).

2. Delete unnecessary motifs or phrases

3. Delete excess chromaticism especially on strong beats.

4. Simplify the melody's shape.

5. Decrease the range. Melodies that cover too wide a range are hard for nonmusicians to grasp. The average listener tends to dismiss what he or she can't understand with minimum effort. A good rule of thumb in pop music is to keep the melodic range within an octave plus a third.

6. Simplify the rhythmic values and syncopation. Try to make the melody more singable and lyrical. It should be relatively streamlined compared to where you began—but not simple-minded.

Here are some more guidelines for melody writing.

1. The more complex or active the harmony, the more obvious the melody should be.

2. The more obvious the harmony, the more complex the melody may be.

3. Any aspect of music that is extremely complex sounds random to the average listener. Avoid extreme complexity.

4. Does the melody have a simple, logical rhythm? Can you sing just the rhythm of the melody?

5. Does the melody fit the chord progression (if you are writing to an existing chord progression)?

6. Do large skips eventually fill themselves in, closing the gap? (This does not have to be immediate.)

7. Does the melody balance predictability with surprise? (This may be subtle or overt.)

8. Practice sketching out the rhythm of the melody; then fill in the notes. Take a rough shape or idea; then refine it.

Repetition

There are three types of repetition.

1. *Exact* where the same melody or motif is repeated throughout. (This is not too common.)

2. *Sequenced* where the motif repeats at different pitches. (See Example 2.6.)

3. *Occasional* where the motif repeats and varies. Variations can be created by extension, inversion, transposition, or rhythmic variation.

Example 2.6: *Melodic Sequences*

Other Characteristics of Melody

There are three basic elements of a melody: (1) interval (the distance between two notes); (2) direction (up, down, and forward); and (3) rhythm. Melody is a horizontal line of notes that has a specific shape and pattern. The horizontal line can occur by steps, where consecutive notes are either a whole or half step apart, or by skip, where consecutive notes are separated by an interval of a minor third or more.

The interval (distance) between the notes that skip is filled in by stepwise motion either up or down. These notes will eventually be heard. This happens in one of two ways. The skip can immediately be filled in (Example 2.7); or the melody skips, continues in the same direction, and soon returns to fill in the skip (Example 2.8). Extensive research has shown that people need to have the skips filled in some times to obtain a sense of completion, fulfillment, or satisfaction. By understanding that need, we can build varying degrees of tension into melodies by determining how and when to fill in the important skips.

Example 2.7: Skip is filled immediately

Example 2.8: Melody continues in direction of skip and eventually fills in

Melody is most effective when tension and release are achieved. This is part of the basic attraction and response to strong melodies. Tension generally is the result of ascending melodies. Release is the result of melodies that descend from the point of tension. Tension builds slowly toward the melodic climax, and release happens quickly (Example 2.9). This curve may occur either by step or by a combination of steps and skips.

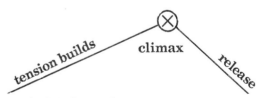

Example 2.9: A melodic curve—tension builds slowly, release occurs somewhat quicker

Melodic content is not an accident but is the result of deliberate choices. Melody notes are derived from *chord tones* (notes from the chord at that moment); *scales,* or modes; *tensions* available

(harmonic and melodic tensions—chord scales; and *embellishments* (notes used for effect that come from outside the key and resolve to chord or scale tones).

EMBELLISHMENTS

There are two types of embellishments—weak and strong. Weak embellishments include the following:

1. A *passing tone*—a nonchord tone that passes between two chord tones up or down, diatonically or chromatically (Example 2.10).

Example 2.10: Passing tones

2. A *neighboring tone*—a nonchord tone that leaves a chord tone by step and immediately returns diatonically or chromatically up or down (Example 2.11).

Example 2.11: Neighboring tones

3. An *anticipation*—a nonchord tone that appears in the melody before the chord to which it belongs. It may tie into an upcoming chord or may be reattacked (Example 2.12).

Example 2.12: Anticipation

4. *Changing tones*—these have two types of indirect resolution (Example 2.13). They can (a) leap from chord tone to nonchord tone and resolve to a chord tone by step or opposite direction, or (b) leap from nonchord tone to nonchord tone and resolve to chord tone by step in the opposite direction.

Example 2.13: Changing tones

5. *Escape tone (échappée)*—a chord tone that moves by step to a nonchord tone (often a nondiatonic note) and is left by a leap in the opposite direction (Example 2.14).

Example 2.14: Escape tones (échapées)

Stong embellishments occur in place of a chord tone and are usually a quarter note in value, depending on tempo. For example, a slow eighth note can equal a moderate quarter note. The following are strong embellishments:

1. *Appoggiatura*—a nonchord tone that occurs on a strong beat. There are two types of appoggiaturas: (a) *prepared,* which are approached by anticipation and resolved by step (Example 2.15); and

(b) *unprepared,* which are approached by leap and resolved by step (Example 2.16).

Example 2.15: Prepared appoggiatura

Example 2.16: Unprepared appoggiatura

2. *Suspensions*—a nonchord tone whose resolution is delayed by a tie. The three basic components of suspension are preparation, suspension, and resolution (to a chord tone) (Example 2.17).

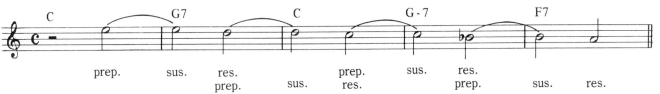

Example 2.17

3. *"Unprepared" suspension*—actually a misnomer, as without preparation, no tone is suspended (Example 2.18).

Example 2.18: Other suspensions

There are two other considerations you should be aware of when writing a melody. First, long notes, notes followed by long rests, and accented or prominent notes almost always are chord tones or available tensions.

Second, melody begins to have harmonic implications when it moves in consecutive skips. When skipping to a note that is not a chord tone, the resolution should be to the nearest chord tone, or the melody begins to imply another tonality.

PHRASES

Melodies contain areas of motion (activity) and areas that are less active. Together these areas define a melody's phrases. A *phrase* is usually played or sung in one breath. An important component of phrasing is space for breath, even on the keyboard or guitar. Each phrase contains its own curve or contour. The release of tension is usually the place for a breath. Melodic shape and *harmonic rhythm* (the phrasing, or cadences, of the chord progression) are often different. For example, a melody may move very slowly in contrast to the chord changes, or vice versa. This is a powerful tool in building tension (Example 2.19).

The same melody will often fit over different or more complex chord progressions. Even though the actual notes remain the same, their relative functions change. This is a powerful way to have continuity while building tension. "One Note Samba," by Jobim, is a good example of this technique (Example 2.20).

Example 2.19: Slow-moving melody—active chord progression

Example 2.20: *Simple two-note melody with increasing harmonic tension*

SECONDARY MELODY, OR COUNTERMELODY

A countermelody moves in contrast to the primary melody. When one moves, the other rests or sustains. For example, in writing background vocals, look for the places where the lead vocal rests to fit in appropriate parts. Singing (in unison or harmony) along with the lead vocal is not a countermelody: it is a thickened primary melody. Countermelody has its own character or personality, independent of the primary melody. Here are the basic elements of a countermelody.

1. It is completely independent. Melody, rhythm, and phrasing are not derived from the primary melody. It can also be an element from some other part of the arrangement.

2. It is directly related. The intervals, direction, and rhythm are same, or very similar, although the starting point in a measure may differ.

3. It is also indirectly related. Only one or two elements resemble the primary melody. The secondary melody has been altered by *augmentation* or *diminution*. (The rhythm or intervals of the melody have been expanded or contracted.) (See Example 2.21.)

Example 2.21: *Typical melody and countermelody*

There are additional considerations for writing melodies and countermelodies.

1. The melody or countermelody may be played or sung in unison combinations, octave unisons, or voiced (thickened).

2. The melody and countermelody are most distinct when different voices or sounds are assigned to each one. When both are in the same register, it is even more important to use different sounds to keep them distinct.

3. Divide the song into sections and phrases. This will help you decide when and where to use a countermelody. Be aware of the primary melody when writing the countermelody.

4. Assign a sound or voice to the melody.

5. Assign a sound or voice to the countermelody.

6. Harmonize primary melody and countermelody when desirable.

7. When the melody moves, the countermelody sustains or rests.

8. When the melody rests, the countermelody moves. The amount of movement of the countermelody is based on two factors. The first factor is the activity of the primary melody. If the primary melody is very active, the countermelody activity should be minimal. If the primary melody is inactive, the countermelody can be more active. The second factor is tempo. The faster the tempo, the less active the countermelody needs to be.

9. In pop music the primary melody and countermelody should be at least a minor third apart when both are attacked simultaneously. Intervals of major or minor seconds between the primary melody and countermelody sound dissonant and obscure the identity of each part.

10. Avoid using altered tensions in the countermelody at the same time the primary melody has unaltered tensions, or vice versa.

11. The primary melody and countermelody should be of contrasting or complimentary tone qualities.

12. If the primary melody is in harmony, the countermelody is most effective in unison or in unison combinations.

13. If the primary melody is at a unison, the countermelody may be harmonized or unison.

When in doubt, write the countermelody in unison and then go back and find the appropriate notes, if any, to harmonize.

14. Use a percussive countermelody. Often a countermelody will be more rhythmic than melodic —almost like punctuation, rather than longer phrases. Percussive backgrounds are often harmonized. Often they "drop in" at specific points when the primary melody rests. It is refreshing to hear an interesting voicing on a percussive countermelody.

Using Your Sequencer

Here are some general thoughts on using a sequencer. These suggestions are designed for a "generic" sequencer. Try all the techniques in this chapter with a variety of sounds.

1. Use your sequencer as a writing workshop. Put any and all versions of your primary melodies and countermelodies on separate tracks. Play them back at all tempos, individually and simultaneously.

2. Compare different versions with the original.

3. Try various quantize functions, including none.

4. Deliberately play melodies back in different time signatures.

5. Compare the retrograde and the retrograde inversion with the original. Play them simultaneously or offset by any given amount.

6. Using two keyboards, transpose one and listen to the same melody (simultaneously) in two keys. Try any or all combinations of keys.

7. Listen to your primary melodies and countermelodies with different patches or combinations of patches.

8. Overdub a track of patch changes so that on every given number of beats of a measure, the timbre changes.

9. Listen to your melody played on a nonpitched sound or a tunable percussion sound. Now you are hearing the rhythmic content of your melody.

10. Thicken (harmonize) any or all of the primary melodies or countermelodies. Try various unison and harmony combinations from within the key, or try any constant or varying intervals. This can create interesting out-of-key harmony notes.

11. Use your countermelody as a new primary melody and write a new countermelody for it.

Chapter Three
Rhythm: Using a
Drum Machine

Drum machines have evolved rapidly in the past few years, particularly in the areas of touch sensitivity, dynamics, and sound quality (ROM and RAM samples). The latest generation of affordable, touch-sensitive, sampling drum machines do away with a lot of the usual criticism about sound and feel. New technology has allowed us to input more emotion into our music than ever possible.

There are people who argue that the whole idea of spending hours getting a machine to do what a great drummer naturally does is absurd. In a certain sense, that's true. Unfortunately, not everyone has access to a good drummer who has great time, expertise in a variety of styles, an arsenal of acoustic and electronic sounds, tireless chops, endless patience, almost perfect memory, and twenty-four-hour availability.

Modern drum machines allow arrangers to work out elements methodically within the rhythmic foundations of their projects. Many musicians and arrangers are becoming sensitive to what drummers do, and therefore they are more skillful at creating solid rhythmic foundations. Drum machines are also great educational tools. By learning to think more like drummers we are better able to communicate our ideas in a drummer's language.

Drum machines, like computers, only do what they are told, and the latest versions are very responsive to input. By understanding groove and feel, we can give more realistic commands to our creative tools. Drum machines are a useful alternative (especially for composition purposes) to actual drums. Judging by the amount of "live" drums on recent recordings and performances, there is no real danger of live drums becoming extinct. For arrangers, a drum machine is a tireless, objective friend and teacher.

Groove and *feel* can be described as the relationship and interaction between the foundation instruments of an arrangement. The real basic part of the groove is between the kick (bass) drum, the snare drum, and the bass line. This is the bottom, or foundation, of most pop arrangements. The next elements are the active parts that move or drive the track. These are the hi-hat, shaker (cabasa), percussion and rhythmic guitar, and keyboard parts. These parts create rhythmic activity and feeling. It's useful to think of parts as either rhythmic or sustained. Sustained parts are in the background and provide contrast and support for the rhythmic foreground. Both are necessary.

Techniques for Programming Drum Machines

When you are first learning to program drum machines, it is best to do some critical and analytical listening. Set aside a period of time each week to analyze drum parts from definitive arrangements in a variety of styles. Transcribe sections from different styles. And, talk to or "hang out" with good drummers whenever possible.

Most drum parts closely (if not exactly) follow the phrase structure of a song. Patterns are usually two to four bars in length. This means that verses, chorus, and bridges will contain repetitions of their respective patterns. Effective programming relies heavily on repetition of basic patterns with occasional variations.

Most pop music has some sort of "back beat" on two and four, usually played by the snare drum. In the beginning of ballads, or quiet sections, the snare is occasionally replaced with a less intense percussive sound (Example 3.1).

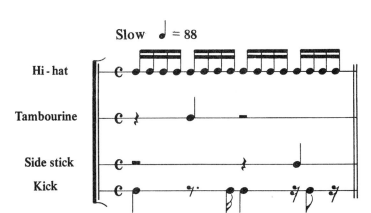

Example 3.1: *Sidestick replaces snare*

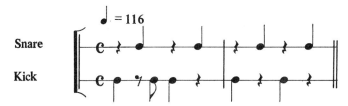

Example 3.2: *Common kick-drum and snare pattern*

Remember that it's better to leave your kick-drum patterns simple at first. This gives you room for options as the arrangement develops. You can always add some kick-drum beats as needed, it's easier than figuring out which ones to remove (Example 3.2).

The hi-hat, cabasa (shaker), ride and crash cymbals, and Latin and ethnic percussion fit around the basic groove. These are the elements that add excitement and motion on top of the foundation. Modern drum machines, especially sampling machines offer authentic versions of almost any drum and percussion sound in ROM and RAM (Example 3.3).

Example 3.3: *The cabasa plays a one-bar phrase within the two-bar pattern*

Usually it's the hi-hat or hi-hat/shaker combination that is the pulse of an arrangement. The most common rhythms are quarter notes, eighths (or eighth-note triplets), sixteenth-note triplets, and occasional thirty-second-note fills. Adding accents to your motion parts (hi-hat/shaker) gives a feeling of realism and excitement. By setting up a pattern of accents you create a subtle "time feel" within the overall time. In Latin music this is called *clave,* and it's a key element in the rhythmic drive. Try the following variations on this basic pattern.

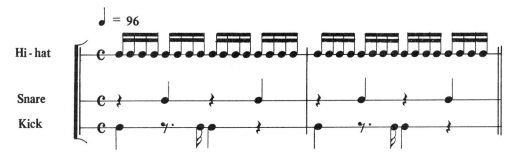

Example 3.4: *Basic pattern*

1. Add accents to your hi-hat part (Example 3.5).

Example 3.5: *Accenting every third hi-hat attack sets up a syncopated time feel within the basic groove*

2. Build a hi-hat part by combining hi-hat and shaker (Example 3.6).

Example 3.6: *Simple doubling of hi-hat part with cabasa provides some thickening but is not really effective*

3. Have hi-hat and shaker play identical parts with different accent patterns (Example 3.7).

Example 3.7: *This pattern of alternating accents makes the parts interesting, and separates them*

4. Have hi-hat and shaker play identical parts, but only one part has accents (Example 3.8).

Example 3.8: *Placing accents in the hi-hat part alone produces a more subtle version of Example 3.7*

5. Have hi-hat and shaker play different rhythms, with only one accented (Example 3.9).

Example 3.9: *Separating two similar parts with space and accents*

6. Have hi-hat and shaker play different rhythms, but both parts have different accents (Example 3.10).

Example 3.10: *Either the hi-hat, shaker, or both are hitting on each sixteenth note*

Omitting certain notes gives the hi-hat part a lighter, more open feeling. Experiment by deleting certain eighth or sixteenth notes. This creates silent accents, or breathing spaces. More realistic parts result. You can really feel the drummer's stick hitting different spots on the hi-hat, accenting or de-emphasizing certain notes. To conclude, accents, omissions, and accents plus omissions create a very realistic feel in the high-pitched instruments (Example 3.11).

Example 3.11: *Pattern with breathing spaces in the motion parts*

There are also some mechanical-technical aspects of most drum machines that can be used to create a realistic feel. Try experimenting with the following:

1. Degrees of swing on any or all parts.

2. Degrees of shuffle.

3. Tuning of any or all drum voices.

4. Clock resolutions—degrees of quantize from none to maximum.

5. Production and signal processing, which is an area to which an entire book could be dedicated. Reverb, panning, gating, delay, and E.Q. have major impact on sound and feel.

6. Dynamic levels—vary the dynamics on different parts.

7. Flams add realism, and allow certain hits to be less perfect, or fatter.

8. Many new drum machines allow panning—the placement of individual drum voices at various points in the stereo image. This creates a feeling of depth, space, and realism.

There is no rigid formula about correct programming. Many great drummers admit that very often keyboard players will create drum parts that drummers would not have considered. There are styles of music that have evolved around the flaws and quirks of drum machines. Some people want a nonhuman, mechanical feeling. As arrangers working in different styles, we really need to know the basics and roots of the styles in which we write. Understanding the basics, (what drummers do and why) gives us the opportunity to make wise, appropriate, and creative choices.

Many of today's records combine drum machines, live-acoustic drums, and various forms of triggered sounds. Drum tracks are often hybrids of old and new technology. Rather than making value judgements, try to learn many approaches and increase your choices. The best drum programs ultimately come from those who really understand what drums can do.

Most people who work alone in their home MIDI studios began their musical involvement on a particular instrument. In many cases they did not begin on drums or drum machines so programming drums does not come as naturally as harmony or writing lyrics. As an arranger, you don't have to be a consummate expert on absolutely every instrument. It helps, but you can try working in collaboration with people who do particular things well. Even though drum parts are the foundation of an arrangement, consider working out other aspects of the arrangement first and then develop the drum parts. Learn to use your sequencer and the tape sync capabilities of your drum machine. If you are working with tape, you can revise and update drum parts as the arrangement grows, if you have

striped the tape with your drum box's (or another device's) sync tone. (There are many books and articles on various styles of syncing to tape or to other devices—for example, sequencers or computers.)

The following is a list of suggestions or approaches to building a solid foundation with your drum machine:

1. Work in two-bar patterns, at least initially.

2. Learn the melodic structure; harmonic rhythm; phrases; form; tempo; and any unusual characteristics, accent patterns, or stylistic implications of the song.

3. Use a basic pattern to generate minor variations for different sections of the arrangement. This way one pattern clones itself, and all the variations come from one source. This process helps build continuity in the basic groove.

4. Change one element of the drum kit at a time so that you have some basis for comparison. The upper-register sounds, like hi-hat or cabasa, often remain the same, while a kick-drum figure changes from section to section, and vice versa.

5. Build a four-bar phrase from two two-bar phrases, an eight-bar phrase from two four-bar phrases, and so forth.

6. Very recent developments in sampling, triggering, and improved decay times have made hi-hats more realistic than ever. If you are not satisfied with your drum machine hi-hats or cymbals after trying everything, consider some live hi-hats or cymbal overdubs.

7. It's often a good idea to leave all but the most critical drum machine fills out of your program until you are sure where the arrangement is going. Almost any instrument is capable of playing slick fills, so wait until you have had a chance to try a few things. You don't always have to keep the groove going under a fill. Let the fill take over, otherwise, it can sound unnatural (like the drummer just grew a few extra arms and legs). The bottom line here is not whether the drum machine can do it; it is how it sounds. Does it sound good, feel good, and fit the music? Short fills work well on top of the groove; longer fills usually need to replace the groove for a few beats to create excitement. When the groove returns, it feels welcome.

8. Most verse, chorus, and bridge sections have their own patterns that don't change radically throughout the arrangement. The groove for the first chorus and last chorus will be almost, if not exactly, the same. If the song changes rhythmically, for example, it might have a half-time feel on the bridge—then the drum groove will change, too. Continuity is important, so design your pattern changes to flow smoothly from section to section.

9. Keep perspective. The drum parts are one of the most important elements in groove and feel but not the only elements. The other rhythm-section instruments and the parts they play have a profound effect on how you ultimately feel the drums. Adding a solid bass line or rhythm guitar can make drum programs sound and feel great. Before trashing your drum machines, or doing unnecessary reprogramming, listen to things in context. Assuming your groove and other parts are solid, you will probably find that the whole is greater than the sum of the parts.

10. Isolate the different parts of the drum program by soloing them on your machine or mixer. Problems can be solved by listening to the elements in isolation. Start with your kick and snare and add one element at a time until the problem shows up. This makes tweaking your parts much easier.

11. Not all the bass-drum hits and bass notes have to coincide. Some will and some won't. However, the bass-drum and bass-line parts do need to be complementary. Accents and important syncopations will probably lock together, but the bass part and kick drum usually retain their own individual characters. They will often be in rhythmic unison, and then they will depart and reunite. Practicing transcription will help you understand this (Example 3.12).

Circled notes coincide with kick-drum part.

Example 3.12: *Kick-drum and bass parts coincide at important points*

12. You don't have to catch every single accent or syncopation in the arrangement with the drums. The drums should catch the major or critical ones. Let the rest go by. This way your drum program serves as a solid base and as a means of contrast for the syncopations around the basic groove. You don't want your drum program to sound like a circus drummer catching every single motion with a cymbal crash. A solid program will be based on the lowest common denominator. Listen to an arrangement where there is a lot of rhythmic activity. More often than not, the drums are the glue that holds everything together. The rest of the arrangement may be syncopated, but the groove underneath is often very simple and provides contrast and reference points for the syncopations.

13. Big, thick sounds impart a solid feeling. If your kick and snare parts are rhythmically correct, but still don't feel right, try the following methods: If the sounds aren't full enough, replace them with fatter sounds or try variations of E.Q., reverb, gating, harmonizers, delay, or tuning. Combine more than one sound to build your snare drum. Two or three snare sounds will often give you the composite sound you need. You can also use different sounds, tunings, and combinations in different sections. In general, only one kick-drum sound is used at a time, but you can experiment.

If your drum sounds are too large, strip away some of the composite layers and work with your E.Q., reverbs, tunings, and miscellaneous outboard gear. Tape speed (if you have vari-speed) is also very effective for changing the pitch and timbre of a sound.

14. Don't be afraid to not use every button, dial, bell, or whistle on your state-of-the-art beat box. If it sounds and feels right, leave it alone. There will be many opportunities to use all the features. ("If it ain't broke, don't fix it.") Manufacturers try to anticipate all your needs, but they assume that your taste will be the final judge.

15. This is not the place to go into a long discussion about drum-sampling techniques, mic placement or signal processing. There are many good articles and books dedicated to that subject. Generally speaking, your drum machine will be able to sample or play back RAM and ROM samples. Most drum machines have trigger ins and outs. This is one way you can use your machine to play the patterns, but use alternate sound sources in place of your existing sounds. Make sure the samples you trigger are appropriate for the music. You can also combine triggered sounds with existing RAM and ROM samples. In this way you can layer many different sounds for specific effects.

16. There are two ways of deleting or adding beats. One way is to add or remove beats, in effect changing the time signature. The other way is to change the groove by silencing one or more beats within a measure but not changing the time signature. This can add elements of surprise, tension, and excitement to an arrangement. The band Tower of Power is famous for creating surprises within the time.

Drum Machine Language

Stepwrite is the mode by which you enter various hits—drum voices—one at a time, without any reference to a metronome. Each drum voice is placed where it should belong in a measure. Hits and rests are entered one at a time until a pattern is established. The most efficient way to do this is to write out the patterns accurately and neatly. When you have entered the patterns, listen back for accuracy and adjust the tempo. This method is especially useful for very complex patterns.

Tapwrite (Realtime) is the most common way of playing or jamming with your drum box. Set up a click for the tempo (time signature), and have an accent on the first beat of each measure or the beginning of the phrase. The accented first beat keeps you on track. Without that beat, it's very easy to enter patterns in a lopsided way. (If all clicks are of equal volume, then there's no reference point.) You can delete the accented first beat whenever you are finished. Determine how long the pattern will be and hit the individual drum keys in real time. Listen back and quantize to taste (if your machine allows you to vary the quantize after the performance).

Once you've worked out all your patterns, *song mode* allows you to link them together in sequence to correspond to the form of the arrangement. Listen back for accuracy, correct number of bars, smooth transitions between sections, relative dynamic balance between drum voices, actual sound of drum voices, and panning (if that's an option). If there are aspects of the overall drum program that need fine tuning, go back to step- or tapwrite and make the adjustments.

Most of the "older" drum machines are not touch-sensitive, but there is a way around that problem. (The word *older* is a relative term these days. *Old* can mean equipment from six months ago.) Use your drum machine as a sound source only. Look in your manual for a way to connect your drum machine via MIDI to a touch-sensitive keyboard and sequencer. Figure 3.1 shows one common way.

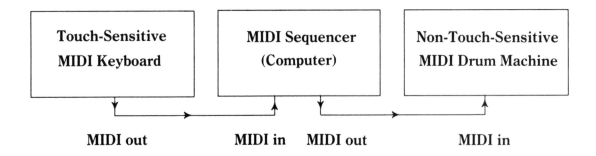

Figure 3.1: *Connecting a drum machine to a touch-sensitive keyboard by MIDI*

You can see from the figure that you play or hit your drum machine by using the keys on your touch-sensitive keyboard. Each drum voice will be assigned (through MIDI) to a key on your instrument. (Check your manuals.) The sequencer remembers the note on-off commands, dynamics, and so on. This allows you to create dynamics, bypass the quantize, or create effects that your drum machine can't do by itself.

Because of specific quantize limitations on some drum machines, you now can program parts the drum machine's computer cannot handle by using this setup. For example, let's say your drum machine can't play sixteenth-note triplets on the hi-hat. By entering this rhythm from your keyboard into the sequencer, you have now got what you want out of the drum box. You now use the sequencer's chain/song-write modes to assemble drum patterns into song form in the same way you assemble keyboard parts/tracks on the sequencer.

CHAPTER FOUR
HARMONY

Harmony is the vertical alignment of three or more notes. We make the distinction between chords (three or more notes) and intervals (two notes). Intervals and chords can be played melodically (one note at a time—arpeggiated) or harmonically (all notes sounding at once). Much of what we consider to be harmonically correct is the result of cultural influence. Our harmonic choices are very different from cultures that use different tunings and scales. A working knowledge of chord progressions and basic voicings is essential for understanding harmony and arranging. (There is a wide choice of excellent books devoted exclusively to modern harmony.)

One of the ways to create interesting arrangements is by using rhythmically activated melody and harmony. There are three basic alterations used.

1. *Anticipation.* A note or chord change is rhythmically anticipated (Example 4.1).

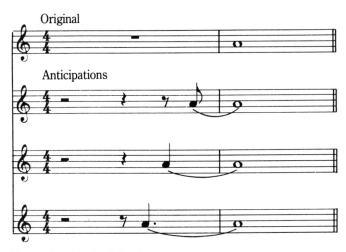

Example 4.1: Anticipation

2. *Delayed attack.* The attack of a note or chord is delayed rhythmically (Example 4.2).

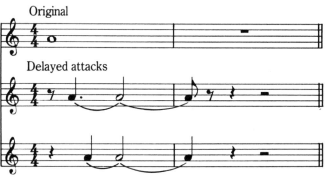

Example 4.2: Delayed attack

3. *Rests.* Anticipations and delayed attacks are used in conjunction with rests (Example 4.3).

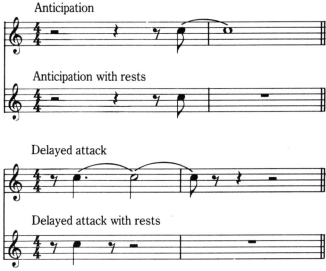

Example 4.3

When rhythmic displacements (anticipations and delayed attacks) are combined with rests, the end result is *syncopation,* or accents on weak beats. (Table 4.1 illustrates strong and weak beats.)

Syncopation

Syncopation is what gives music its rhythmic character. By accenting notes on weak beats or by moving notes to weak beats and then accenting them, melody and chord progressions gain new rhythmic life (Example 4.4).

TABLE 4.1.

Strong and Weak Beats in Various Time Signatures

Time Signature	Strong Beats	Weak Beats
$\frac{4}{4}$	1 and 3, 2 and 4	up beats
$\frac{3}{4}$	1, 2, and 3	up beats
$\frac{2}{4}$	1 and 2	up beats
$\frac{6}{8}$	1 and 4	2, 3, 4, and 6

Example 4.4

In writing syncopation, it is important to be aware of the invisible bar line. This is the imaginary line that separates the two halves of the bar. In $\frac{4}{4}$ time, beats 1 and 2 should be clearly separated from beats 3 and 4. Using a tie is the only way a note can sound across an invisible bar line (Example 4.5). Not all music is in $\frac{4}{4}$ time so there should be a way of subdividing compound rhythms. Part of an arranger's task is to anticipate confusion and indicate solutions. A compound time signature can be subdivided in at least two ways. Subdividing your parts correctly means quicker, more accurate results and better communication (Example 4.6).

Example 4.5: *Invisible bar lines*

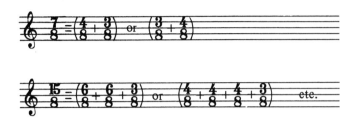

Example 4.6: *Subdividing compound time signatures*

Tensions

Tensions are the notes above the fifth of the chord. Although sevenths are chord tones (notes within the first octave of the chord), they are also tensions. It is important to understand tensions to (1) analyze melody for its harmonic implications and (2) choose the notes from which to build chords.

Here's a real-world example of why knowing chords and scales is important. Let's assume you are in the key of C and there's a B♭7(♯11) chord for four bars. You want to write an eighth-note ascending violin line while sustaining the lower string parts. Knowing the notes in the chord and scale allows you to solve the vertical and horizontal problems with confidence, instead of guessing which notes to use. (See Example 4.7.)

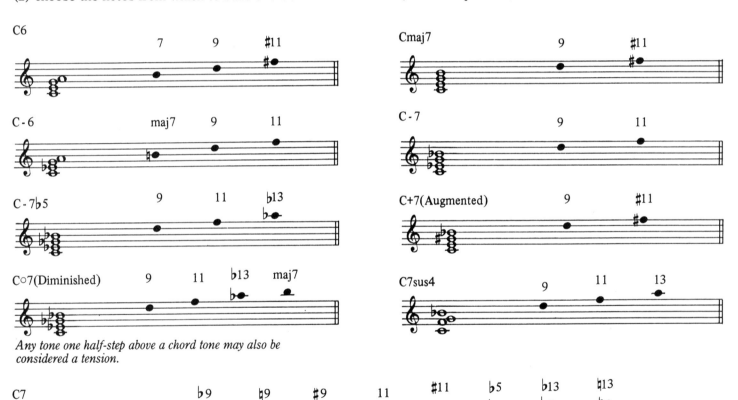

Any tone one half-step above a chord tone may also be considered a tension.

Example 4.7: *Melodic tensions*

Example 4.8 lists the chord scales used in almost all pop or jazz harmonic situations. They are referenced to the key of C. It is a good idea to practice writing them out in all twelve keys. This takes a little time, but it quickly becomes a reflex. Knowing how to voice a D9 chord is great, but A♭9 is just as valid. Work on one key per day.

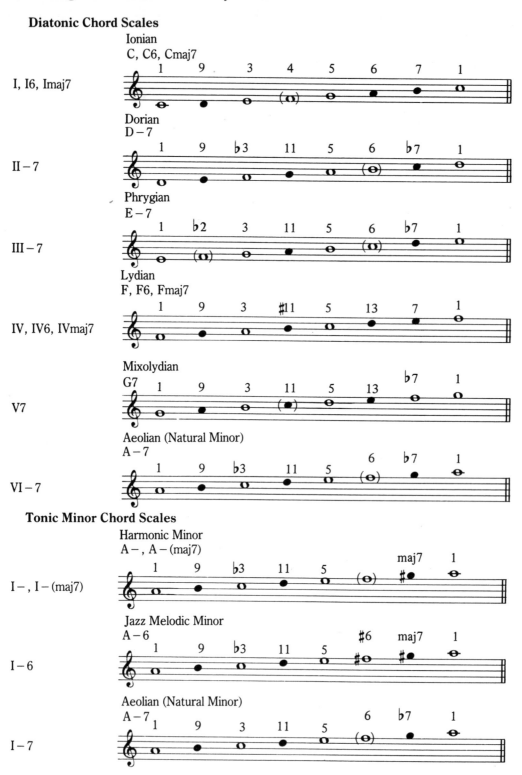

Example 4.8: *Chord scales (● = tension; notes in parentheses are passing tones not used in constructing chord voicings)*

Example 4.8 *(continued)*

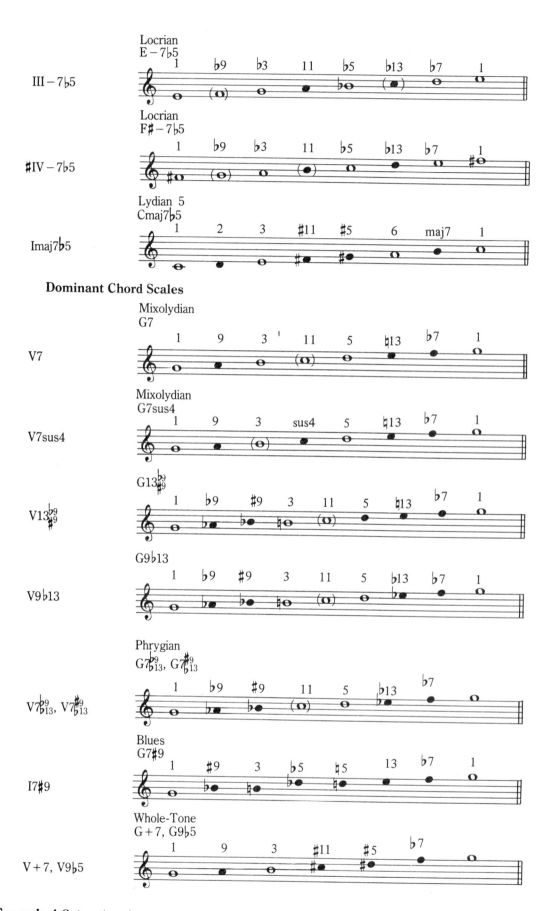

Dominant Chord Scales

Example 4.8 *(continued)*

The altered scale contains the same tones as a Lydian♭7 scale a tritone away.

By the same token, the chords G7alt and D♭7♯11 are identical. Very often you will see G7/D , which is the same as D♭7♯11; or D♭7/G, which is the same as G7alt.

Example 4.8 (continued)

TABLE 4.2.

Reference Guide to V7 Chord Scales.

Chord	Scale
V7 of I (G7 ⇨ C) V7 of IV (C7 ⇨ F) V7 of V (D7 ⇨ G7)	Any type of Dominant chord scale
V7 of II − (A7 ⇨ D −) V7 of III − (B7 ⇨ E −) V7 of VI − (E7 ⇨ A −	Any Dominant chord scale with ♭13 (♯5)
V7 to I − (G7 ⇨ C −)	Any Dominant chord scale with ♭13 (♯5)
♭II7 (D♭7) or any tritone substitution for a V7 chord	Lydian ♭7 Scale
V + 7 (G + 7)	Whole-Tone Scale
V7sus4 (G7sus4)	Mixolydian Scale
I7♯9 (C7♯9)	Blues Scale

TABLE 4.3.

Tension Substitutions.

Chord Type	Tension Substitution Options
Major 6	9 for 1 maj7 for 6
Major 7	9 for 1
Minor 6	9 for 1
Minor 7	9 for 1*
Dominant 7	9 for 1 ♭9 for 1 ♯9 for 1 ♭5 for 5 13 for 5 ♭13 (♯5) for 5

*except for III − 7 chords when 9 is not available (see Example 4.8: Chord Scales)

Background Writing

Before looking at the types of voicings and their constructions, it is useful to examine some important considerations that apply to harmony and more specifically, background writing.

1. When the melody moves, the harmony sustains. This sounds obvious, but how often do you find yourself forgetting the melody when you are working on the harmonic rhythm or voicings?

2. An active melody demands minimal activity in the harmonic rhythm.

3. The faster the tempo, the less active the harmonic rhythm.

4. Keep the background voicings in a register that doesn't conflict with the melody.

5. Decide on a dynamic level for the background voicings. This is particularly critical when working with samples or synth patches that sound best only at certain levels. A horn stab sample, which sounds great high and loud, will sound unnatural if played soft and low. When choosing sounds for your voicings, consider the dynamics as well.

6. The top note of the voicing should not clash with the melody. Avoid half steps and major seconds between the top two notes of the voicing.

7. The timbre of the background should contrast with or complement the melody. This usually means different textures or families of sounds between the melody (foreground) and background.

There are several common varieties of backgrounds. Although we are not outlining specific voicings yet, the following types of backgrounds occur most often:

1. *Sustained backgrounds*—voicings written for the middle register of an instrument. These are often called *pads,* and they are rhythmically inactive, in support of active parts (Example 4.9).

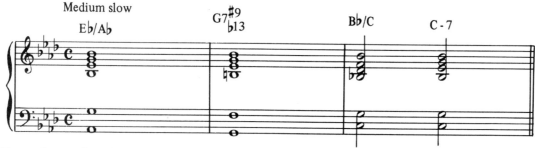

Example 4.9: *Sustained pad voicing*

2. *Percussive* or *active backgrounds*—rhythmically active parts that provide energy or motion under the melody. They are often harmonized, and the type of voicing depends on the range of the melody and the type of sounds being used in the voicing (Example 4.10).

Example 4.10: *Active background*

3. *Linear backgrounds*—single lines (not voiced) that clearly outline the harmony. Common types of linear backgrounds involve simple lines, motifs, or melodies that use the thirds and sevenths of chords or other notes characteristic of the chord (Example 4.11).

Example 4.11: *Linear background*

4. *Original motifs*—chord tones, tensions, or approach notes. These are either unison or voiced. Again, check the melody. If the melody is unison, harmonized motifs make for good contrast. If the melody is harmonized, try unison on the background motifs. Any of these techniques can and should be tried in various combinations. For example, a sustained pad part may become active in places when the melody rests.

Voicings

Always plan a course of action, phrase by phrase, section by section. Know where you are going so you can build toward climax points in a logical way. Here are some specific techniques to determine the types of voicings to use.

1. Check the range and register of the melody. Is the melodic range wide or narrow? This helps you find the general register for the backgrounds.

2. Figure out approximate top and bottom notes in the voicings.

3. Look for common tones between chords and for possible voice leadings to make smooth transitions.

4. Now that you have tentatively outlined a top and bottom note for the voicing(s), plan the middle voices. Avoid too many leaps, skips and abrupt movement in the inner voices. A good rule of thumb is that inner voices (notes between the top and root) should not move more than the melody plus a major second. This means that if the melody moves from C up to F (a perfect fourth), no inner voice should move more than a perfect fifth. The reason for this rule is simple: The motion of the inner voices should not overshadow or distract attention from the melody. Analyze the intervals in the melody and carefully choose top notes for the voicings that allow room for smooth motion from voicing to voicing (Example 4.12).

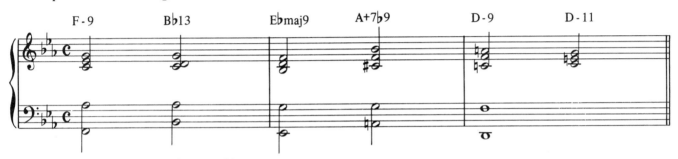

Example 4.12: Inner voices moving smoothly

5. The bottom note in a voicing usually is the root, fifth, passing tone, pedal note, or ostinato. Before constructing specific bass lines or melodic bass parts, determine the exact type of chord(s) (major, minor, dominant, and so forth) and the root that will be incorporated into a bass part or bass line.

Construct a bass line that moves melodically as well as harmonically. Writing bass notes that only outline the roots of the chords may be sufficient, but work at developing bass lines with melodic character (Example 4.13).

Example 4.13

6. The top note in a voicing must be an available chord tone or tension and should outline a logical pattern. In a sense, the top notes have their own subtle melodic contour. They should follow a rising, descending, or other recognizable pattern.

7. Open voicings (which go beyond the scope of two octaves) are best for the high points of a melody.

8. Close-position voicings work best in support of a melody's lower notes. Extremes in register often sound best as unisons.

9. A simple chord can take on new life when some higher partials of the harmonic series are added in the high register in a different timbre.

10. Voicings sound richest when there are no unusual gaps between voices.

11. If the background voicings are primarily pads, the choice of sound is critical. The sounds and voicing are everything since the part is rhythmically inactive. The sound(s) themselves become the critical element in the part.

12. When you are searching for the sounds for your voicings, start with a reason for combining particular sounds.

In creating the voicings for your harmonies, it is critical to balance the voicing, no matter what type. All the notes do not have to work under your fingers on the keyboard. Following the spacing of the harmonic series and observing the low interval limits will help you construct the most resonant voicings. Remember that a voicing played on acoustic piano may not work on strings, brass, or some fantastic MIDI synth patch.

The power of MIDI allows for any deliberate or random combination of sounds. Relate a voicing to a particular sound, and the sound to a part. Never assume that a voicing with one sound (or combination of sounds) will automatically work with other sounds.

Allow time for trial and error while switching patches on the same voicing. Enter the voicings into your sequencer and either program patch changes and combinations or do the changes manually. The shape of the voicing should follow the order of partials in the *harmonic series* (Example 4.14).

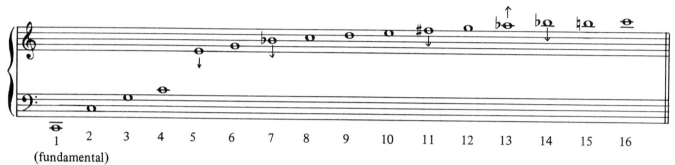

(fundamental)
↓ *These tones are slightly flat compared to equal temperament.*
↑ *This tone is slightly sharp compared to equal temperament.*

Example 4.14: *Order of partials in the harmonic series*

The sound should relate to the part, and the range of individual and combined sounds is often governed by acoustic considerations. As an example of this last point, Example 4.15 shows the points below which specific intervals lose their clarity and sound "muddy."

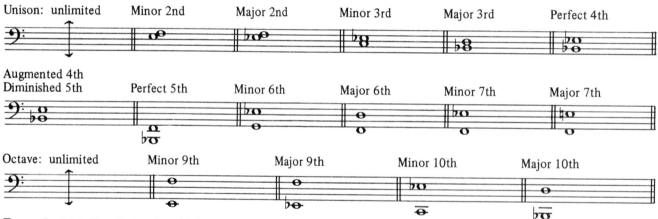

Example 4.15: *Low limits of specific intervals*

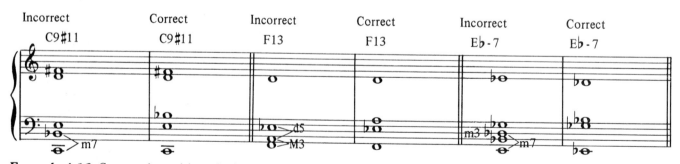

Example 4.16: *Common low-voicing mistakes*

Play through the sample voicings in Examples 4.15 and 4.16 using different sounds and combinations of sounds. Careful study of these examples will help keep the low end of your voicings out of the mud.

Although there are distinctions between keyboard and other voicings, many are multipurpose or utility voicings. They serve a variety of purposes on and off the keyboard. Keyboard voicings have traditionally been considered to be piano voicings. Now that keyboards are used to produce every conceivable sound, it's much more important to understand the acoustic instruments that can also play the voicings. Effective voicings have instruments, voices, and sounds playing on notes characteristic of a style and part. Sometimes this involves writing sounds to play in extreme registers. For example, many pop horn sections have a baritone sax playing in its lowest register, with trumpets playing high notes. The voicing may be a spread, or in fourths, or in octave unisons. The most common multipurpose voicings are closed position, drop 2, drop 2 + 4, drop 3, spreads, fourths, and clusters. We'll examine each type a little later on in this chapter.

The Harmonic Series

The harmonic series has been mentioned a number of times in this text, and it is important to offer a definition and explanation. Any vibrating medium, whether it's a column of air, string, digital, or analog representation of a sound, produces a predominant fundamental sound. Play a low C on your keyboard, and you will hear that note as well as other notes of less intensity that are present in that initial note. These additional tones are called *harmonics, partials,* or *overtones* of the fundamental. These partials, although not always audible, are always present and are in a fixed mathematical ratio to the *frequency* (pitch) of the fundamental. Their presence has much to do with the timbre of that fundamental.

In theory, this series of partials extends to infinity. In western music we utilize the fundamental (F) and the next fifteen partials. The F generates a series of whole-number multiples. Any numerical ratio (and any interval) may be expressed using the terms of the series. For example, the interval of the octave (F to the next note up) may be expressed as 1:2, the fifth (C to G) as 2:3, the major third as 4:5, and the minor third as 5:6.

As we go upward through the series, the intervals (distance) between partials become smaller as the rates of vibrations (frequencies) are closer together. Note that the fundamental pitch is present in every octave of the series. The octave of any note in the series is always a power of two going up or a reciprocal power of two (going down).

$F \times 2^1 = F \times 2 = F$ one octave higher

$F \times 2^2 = F \times 4 = F$ two octaves higher

$F \times \frac{1}{2} = F$ one octave lower

$F \times \frac{1}{2}^2 = F$ two octaves lower

The *fundamental* is the note that generates the intervals. The intervals, as nature creates them, have

been modified by our even-tempered tuning system. In nature some of the intervals are out of tune compared to the way we adjust them. We have made a compromise with nature to please our ears. The twelve notes of the octave-tuning system contain all the partials in the series. Any note in a voicing generates harmonics of its own, however, for our purposes the lowest note (usually the root) is considered the fundamental in anyvoicing. The lower the F, the more harmonics there are in audible range. We play roots in low registers to give the harmonics a chance to be used or heard in their natural places in our voicings.

The tone quality of a human voice in falsetto is similar to that of a guitar with a capo placed halfway up its neck. The string begins to vibrate at its halfway point, reducing the amount of harmonics. This is often why chords sound unnatural when voiced too high. There are not as many partials sounding. The F has been placed in a higher octave, reducing the amount of partials available in audible range.

We have avoided using the word *overtone* because it can be misleading. The word implies that one note is "over" the next, when the real comparison involves the note to its fundamental only. The note is generated by the F, not its adjacent lower neighbor. All partials relate to the F. In a C7 chord, the B-flat is the flat seventh of C7, not the flat third of G (the fifth partial). In developing voicings, it is useful to relate all the notes to the root F and to follow the spacing of the harmonic series to get maximum richness. The higher you go, the closer together the notes are.

Another term worth defining is resonance. *Resonance* comes from "resound," which means "to sound again." This is similar to mechanical feedback. A particular substance vibrates at the same frequency as the source. This is sympathetic vibration, or resonance. When secondary vibrations audibly reinforce the source by sympathetic vibration, resonance occurs. Part of a great string sound (either live, synthesized, or sampled), is the inherent characteristic of resonance. Much of the beauty in sound comes from the source interacting sympathetically (for example, through the effects of the instrument or room) or artificially (for example, with reverb or ambience). The resonance of a voicing is derived from the notes sympathetically vibrating with their fundamental, with each other, with the body of the instrument, and with the immediate environment.

Sounds, chords, or intervals are often described as being consonant or dissonant. These are relative terms. An interval or voicing that is consonant in one situation may be dissonant in another or vice versa. Context plays a key role in our subjective response to sounds. Consonance evokes a feeling of relative stability, and dissonance evokes relative instability.

The word *relative* is also subject to cultural conditioning. Music of some cultures may sound dissonant to our ears, but these cultures may simply be using the harmonic series in different ways. The harmonic series is universal; however, the applications are cultural. We tend to use a modified version of the first fifteen partials; other cultures voice their chords based on different combinations that are often built on the upper end of the series. This can produce different systems of tuning and temperament.

Low-interval limit violations can be described as two or more notes placed too close together to retain their individual characters. We sometimes deliberately play intervals or clusters of notes below the low-interval limits for special effects and drama. This is more common in nonpop music of the twentieth century. For examples, listen to Bartók, Stravinsky, or Hindemith.

When you combine timbres, remember that you combine them for a reason. Be deliberate and organized. Try to have a general idea of the sounds you want to combine. Categorizing and storing sounds by family helps in assembling voicing menus. If the sounds don't necessarily correlate to acoustic instruments, make up your own names or categories (for example, special effects, cloud sounds, or warm pads).

Examples of Common Voicings

The following pages give examples of the most common voicings, along with explanations and suggestions. The voicings are generic in that they work in most situations, and they are illustrated without regard to specific orchestration. The context you work in will help you choose and orchestrate voicings. A variety of styles, lots of transcription, analytical listening, score analysis, and trial and error are major factors in learning to write effective voicings. You can also do everything right, have it sound great, and the client or artist who has hired you can say he or she does like it or wants an entirely different approach. That's life, so have some alternatives.

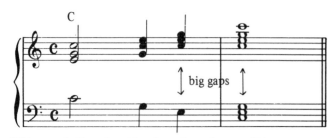

This sounds fine when played on piano, but would be poor spacing for a string or brass ensemble.

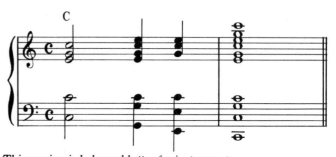

This version is balanced better for instruments.
Example 4.17: *Typical keyboard voicing problem and solution*

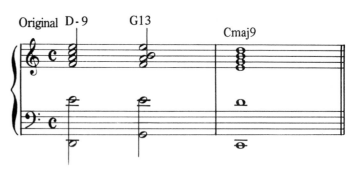

Drop 2 voicing: Open up the original voicing by dropping the second highest voice one octave

Drop 3 voicing: Open up the original voicing by dropping the third highest voice one octave

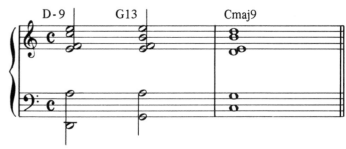

Drop 2 + 4: Open up the original voicing by dropping the second and fourth highest voices one octave

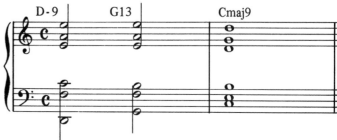

Example 4.18: *This is a typical closed-position voicing and its possible variations*

When you open up a closed-position voicing by using either the drop 2 or the drop 2 + 4 technique demonstrated in Example 4.18, you can add some color to the voicing by using an available tension in the place of the "new" second and fourth voices (Example 4.19).

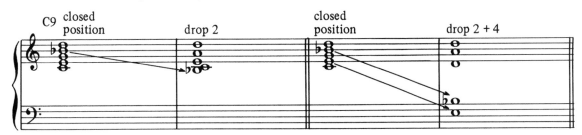

Example 4.19

Example 4.20 shows various spread voicings, which are effective in harmonizing sustained or percussive melodies and general background harmonies. The full sound of a chord is achieved by combining chord tones and available tensions at logical spacings. Try writing your own examples and entering them into a sequencer. Be sure to check low interval limits and spacing. Mix and combine various sounds on the same voicing. Spreads are also useful if your keyboards are being split and the amount of available voices is limited. Spread voicings are commonly used in pad parts.

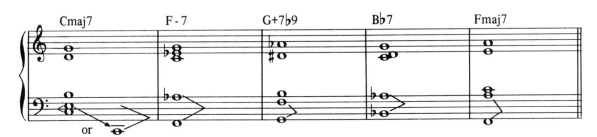

Example 4.20: *Spread voicings*

Table 4.4 indicates the correct spacing between notes in five-part spread voicings such as those shown in Example 4.20. Keeping the notes within these ranges holds the overall character of the voicing together. Using wider spacings than those indicated can cause the notes to no longer sound like part of the voicing. Keeping the notes within range adds maximum resonance, allowing you to create a very full, rich sound with a minimum of notes.

TABLE 4.4.

Maximum Distances Between Notes in a Spread Voicing.

melody note (chord tone or tension)	1	
		octave or less
supporting chord tone or tension	2	
		octave or less
third or seventh	3	
		octave or less
third or seventh	4	
		tenth or less
root	5	

Example 4.21 demonstrates the use of spread voicings to create backgrounds in three typical contexts.

Sustained melody

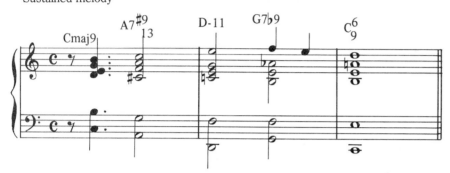

Percussive melody

Background for sustained melody

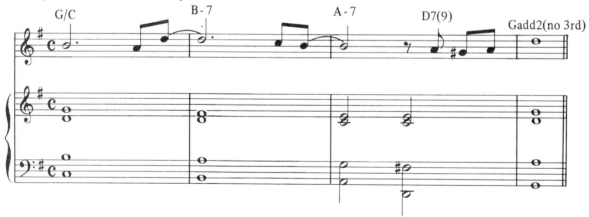

Example 4.21: *Harmonization of melody with spread voicings*

Example 4.22 shows additional voicings for dominant chords with tensions in the melody voice. These voicings allow for more resonance or tension and can be applied in a wide range of contexts. Again, enter them in a sequencer and assign different sounds.

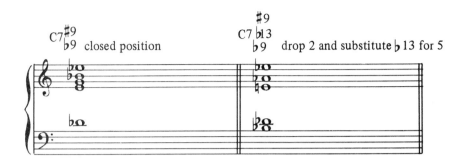

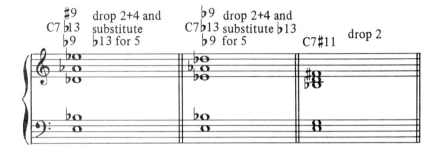

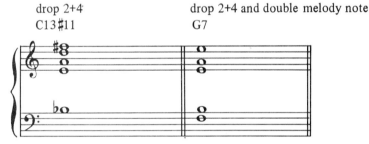

Example 4.22

FLAT-NINTH INTERVALS

Minor-ninth (flat-ninth) intervals in voicings should be avoided. When you are working out voicings, you will probably end up with some that look fine on paper. However, a flat-ninth interval between the bottom note and top note of the voicing can be disturbing. The reason is that you have placed certain notes out of their natural order in the harmonic series. You will usually voice the thirds and sevenths lower in the chord than tensions. When you reverse their order, flat-ninth intervals may occur. You can generally avoid this by supporting tensions with thirds and sevenths (the lower partials) in lower voices. One common exception to this rule is the V7♭9, which has, as its basic nature, the flat-ninth interval (Table 4.5).

If you are playing voicings on a relatively neutral-sounding patch (for example, a DX-7 Rhodes), the flat-ninth intervals may not jump out as much because the sound itself minimizes the dissonance. This does not make the voicings any more correct. The same voicings played on other patches or by

TABLE 4.5.

Minor Ninth (♭9) Intervals to Avoid in All Chord Voicings.

Chord Type	Interval to Avoid	
Major 7	root	♭9
	7	
Minor 6	3	♭9
	7	
Minor 7	3	♭9
	7	
Dominant 7	11 ♭13 ♭7	♭9
	3 5 13	
but		
Dominant 7	♭9	♭9 OK
	root	

acoustic instruments can really obviate the harshness. So don't count on the smoothness of a sound to cover up any voicing flaws. Example 4.23 illustrates common flat-ninth violations and practical solutions.

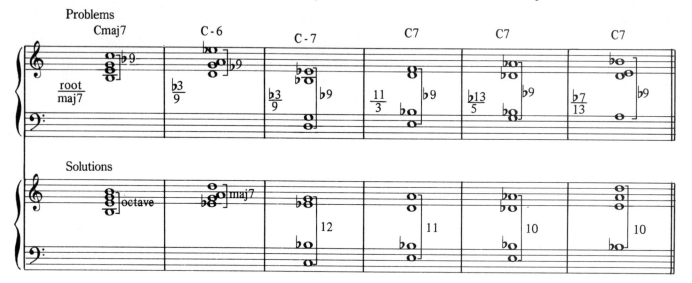

Example 4.23: *Flat-ninth voicing problems*

CORRECT VOICING AND VOICE LEADING

Background harmony parts are usually written by combining a number of voicing types. The style of the music, its melodic and rhythmic content, and types of chords will help you make the necessary decisions. For example, voicings that sound good on a lush pop arrangement may not be stylistically appropriate for a hard-rock song. Correct voicing has to do with (1) physical construction and (2) appropriateness for the style (regardless of how correct the voicings are). Give equal consideration to both.

Spend lots of time listening and transcribing. Keep a workbook of different voicings and put them in your sequencer. Listen back using various sounds, splits, and combinations. A good way to develop arranging technique is to see how many different background harmonies, parts, or voicings you can develop for one song. Let the song be a vehicle for your experiments.

Examples 4.24 and 4.25 combine several voicing types, yet the transitions are smooth. Good voice leading helps hold chord changes together. Voice leading essentially means that voices lead (move) smoothly, following the path of least resistance to the next chord. An abrupt change in voicings or registers can work well when you want that particular effect. This is usually done in transition sections or for the creation of dramatic effect. Just be sure that you are in control and that the voicings are not running away from you. A good way to plan smooth voice leading is to pick the climax points (or important chords), voice them first, and then work backwards toward the beginning of the phrase or section. If you have voiced the critical places first, it's much easier to plan a course of action.

Example 4.24

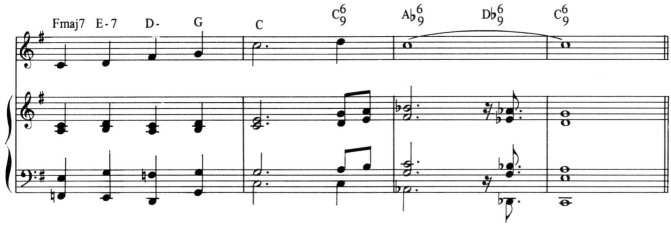

Example 4.24(continued)

Voicings in Fourths

With voicings in fourths, the predominant interval between adjacent notes is a fourth (usually a perfect fourth). Dominant chords will always contain the tritone (augmented fourth) except in the case of the V7sus4. The interval between the top two voices may also be a third. This interval on top of the voicing gives warmth to the open or percussive nature of a voicing in fourths. These voicings have an immediately recognizable sound, and they are very powerful. They are particularly effective for percussive or punchy sections, horn stabs, sustained harmonic areas, and active or syncopated parts. Due to the nature of their construction, voicings in fourths can make an ordinary chord sound different or special. They provide a very powerful technique when you want a section to sound reharmonized, without actually altering the harmony. Because the perfect fourth is not a predominant interval in the harmonic series, voicings in fourths can be ambiguous, implying several chords or tonalities simultaneously. Voicings in fourths can give an ordinary chord progression new energy.

Example 4.25

Chord Symbols

The labeling of chord symbols is a subject of controversy among musicians, but it really shouldn't be. There is a way to write chord symbols that is clear, logical, and that everyone will understand. The correct or best way is simply the one that any musician can interpret without confusion.

Table 4.6 is a chart of chord symbols, written in the most logical, clear way. Also included are common versions that are misleading or ambiguous. There is nothing more frustrating than not being able to communicate ideas because the symbols don't work effectively.

If a chord symbol, for example C7(13), has a thirteenth, the highest number in the parentheses always implies the lower, supporting tensions. A thirteenth implies the available elevenths, ninths, and sevenths. Natural tensions imply other natural tensions. Altered tensions imply other altered tensions. A $V7(^{b9}_{13})$ has a flat ninth, and a natural thirteenth as the available tensions. The specific tensions should be noted clearly in the parentheses. Elevenths in V7 chords replace the thirds. A natural eleventh (equalling sus4) will not be used simultaneously with a third in a V7 chord, and a V7 chord with a third will not contain a natural eleventh (sus4).

TABLE 4.6
Chord Symbols.

Clear		Ambiguous	
C7, C7(9), C9, $C7(^9_{13})$, C13, C7($\sharp$11), $C7(^{\sharp9}_{13})$, C13$\sharp$11, C7$\flat$9, etc.	C7̸	A 7 with a slash through it is sometimes used to indicate a major seventh chord.	
	C7−9, $C7^{-9}_{-13}$	At a glance, these symbols might seem to indicate minor chords.	
Cmaj7, Cmaj9, Cmaj7$\sharp$11, Cmaj7($\sharp$11), Cmaj7$\flat$5, C6, C^6_9, etc.	C7̸, CM7	Either of these symbols may be mistaken for a minor chord.	
	CΔ7	The triangle may be mistaken for a degree sign (°) which indicates a diminished chord.	
C−7, C−9, C−11, C−9(11), etc.	Cmin7, Cm7	These are OK if your handwriting is extremely neat, but the minus sign (−) is clearest.	
C−7$\flat$5, C−7$\flat$5(11), C−7($\flat$5), etc.	C⌀7	Although this is a standard symbol for half-diminished (another name for minor seventh flat five), as many people will be stumped by it as will recognize it.	
C+7, Caug7, C+9, etc.			
C°, C°7	Cdim7	This could be mistaken for Cdom(inant)7.	
Cadd2, C2(no3rd), Csus2		These are not to be confused with ninth chords which contain a seventh. Cadd2 is made up of the notes C, D, E, and G. Cadd 2 (no 3rd) or Csus2 is made up of the notes C, D, and G.	
Cmaj7$\sharp$11	Cmaj7$\sharp$4	This is confusing because a sharp-four chord does not contain a seventh or a ninth. If this is the chord you want, you should use C($\sharp$4).	
Cmaj7$\sharp$5		This is not to be confused with C7$\flat$13 which contains a perfect fifth.	

The following steps will help you construct voices in fourths.

1. Determine from which chord scales the notes are coming. Analyze the chord progression, chord symbols, and functions. This is very important. An E − 7 chord has different notes in the key of C than it does in G or D.

2. Voice down from the melody note, or top note, spacing the available notes by perfect fourths. Use occasional thirds, fifths, and tritones as needed. For example, you may find that placing a third between the two top notes allows you to have more fourths in the remaining lower voices. You can construct fourth voicings from the bottom up, but in this type of voicing top to bottom is usually more effective, at least until the technique becomes second nature for you.

3. Avoid adjacent thirds. They tend to negate the overall sound or flavor of the fourth voicings. A stack of fourths has a totally different sound than a stack of thirds.

4. Avoid doubling notes until the voicing becomes larger than five notes.

5. Avoid flat-ninth intervals, for all the reasons previously discussed.

6. All V7 chords (except V7sus4) must contain the tritone (third and seventh).

7. It is all right for a voicing not to contain the root. The root may be played by some other instrument or sound, or it can be implied. If you have been in the same key for a while, chances are that you have established the tonality and implanted the root in the listener's ear, so don't worry about having roots in every single fourth voicing. The purpose of these voicings is to change color. As long as the basic chord sound is there (even if implied or previously established), it is okay.

8. Since fourth voicings are widely spaced, they work best when there are no radical leaps in register. Good voice leading is still important. These are fairly rich voicings and should move smoothly. In general, the more rich or dense a voicing, the more attention it calls to itself. If you move by large skips, it will be very obvious. If that's the effect you want, okay; if not, follow the previous guidelines for smooth voice leading. Example 4.26 shows various fourth voicings.

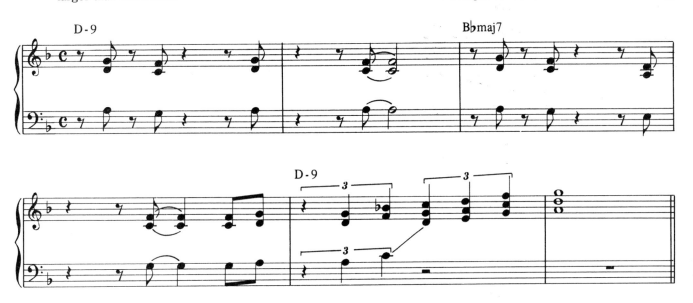

Example 4.26

9. *Approach notes* (notes between chords) can be harmonized in fourths, or they can be left alone without being harmonized. Example 4.27 shows ways to handle approach notes.

10. *Constant structures* are voicings whose intervallic structures and relationships remain identical from chord to chord. This is akin to using exactly the same type of voicing as you move through a chord progression; the notes change but the intervallic relationships remain the same. Voicings in fourths are perfect for constant structures since they have such a distinct sound. Constant-structure fourth voicings are very effective in building tension over a pedal point or ostinato. Constant structures over pedals and ostinati often involve out-of-key or chromatic passing notes in the voicings. The overall sound and the cadences are most important. (Example 4.28 shows constant structures over pedal points, including harmonized chromatic passing notes.)

Original

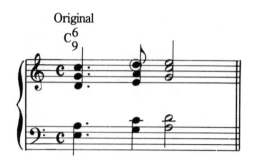

Parallel approach

using chord a whole step below   *using chord a whole step above*

Dominant approach

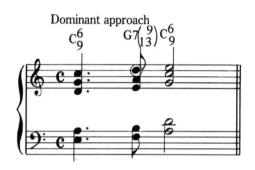

Independent lead

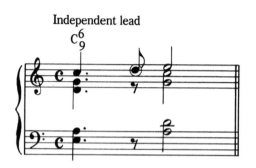

Example 4.27: *Reharmonization of approach notes*

Diatonic

Diatonic and chromatic

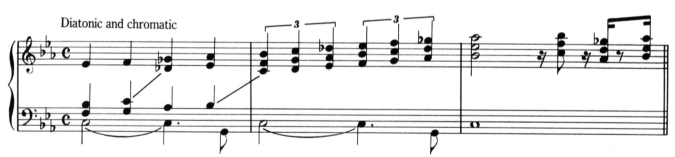

Example 4.28: *Constant structures over a pedal point*

Clusters

Clusters are voicings where the predominate interval between adjacent notes is a second (major or minor). Like fourth voicings, this type of voicing has its own unique and immediately recognizable sound. The following are considerations to use when constructing clusters.

1. Determine the chord scale and analyze the chord progression and melody. Voice down from the melody using available chord tones or tensions spaced a second apart, and when necessary, use a third between adjacent voices.

2. Avoid a minor second between the top two notes. The melody note can often be separated from the rest of the voicing by a third or fourth.

3. Try to have at least one minor second in the voicing but not between the top two notes.

4. Observe the low-interval limits for seconds. Clusters below the low-interval limits sound really muddy. This is occasionally good for a special effect but not for clarity in the voicing.

5. Cluster voicings do not have to contain roots as long as the basic chord sound is there.

6. Clusters work very well on the lower notes of a melodic passage where tension is desired, and spacing between notes is limited by the already low range. This is a ready-made situation for clusters.

7. Clusters are very effective for percussive backgrounds, horn stabs, rhythmic punctuation, and for rich sustained parts (for example, pads).

8. Clusters work well on high melody notes to add tension and brilliance.

9. Due to their dense nature, be careful in using clusters or constant-structure clusters on rapidly moving eighth-note passages. This may work as a special effect but it often blurs the melody. Consider the tempo before using clusters on rapidly moving eighth notes.

10. Clusters work well when mixed with other types of voicings.

Example 4.29 gives a variety of cluster voicings and applications.

Comparison of third, fourth, and cluster voicings

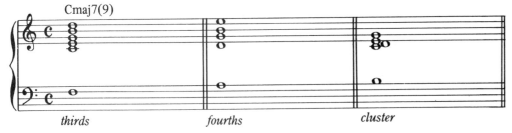

thirds   *fourths*   *cluster*

Various cluster voicings

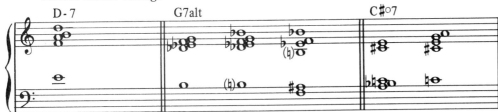

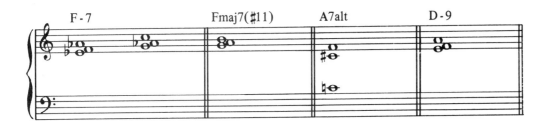

Example 4.29

Upper-Structure Triads

Upper-structure triads (USTs) are major, minor, and occasionally augmented triads that are chord tones or tensions of the chord being voiced. USTs can be thought of as triads containing higher partials of the harmonic series that are part of a chord or chord scale. At least one tension should be part of a UST in order to be most effective. USTs can contain octave doublings of notes already in the voicings.

The following is a list of suggestions for using USTs:

1. Analyze the melody, the chord progression, and determine appropriate chord scales.

2. Use the melody note as the root, third or fifth of a triad in close position. If the melody note is already a tension of the chord, build the triad around it from other available tensions or chord tones. There are often several choices of notes for USTs, especially on altered dominant chords.

3. Support the UST with a voicing that contains the basic chord sounds (root, third, seventh, and so forth).

4. The bottom note of a UST should be no more than an octave away from the rest of the voicing and not closer than a minor third. More than an octave separation creates an unbalanced or poor voicing, and less than a minor third defeats the sound of it being a separate UST. A UST less than a minor third away from the voicing is no longer a UST. It's just part of the voicing, which may contain the same notes.

5. After selecting the notes for the UST, support it with a voicing that contains the basic chord sound or a voicing in fourths. Voicings in fourths work well with USTs and create rich, full sounds. Again, don't consider this in isolation. Your choice of voicings must support the whole piece of music. Some voicings just don't sound well or appropriate in certain styles, no matter how "hip" they are.

6. USTs are good for stressing high points within or at the ends of phrases. They are effective for ending chords and add character to punchy or percussive passages.

7. Some situations are ready-made for USTs in that the melody has an arpeggiated version of notes available for USTs.

8. USTs work well over pedal points or ostinato. In this way you can imply the chord sound without fully voicing the chord. This is a strong technique for exposing the harmony of a song in a new or fresh way. It works well in open or breakdown sections of an arrangement.

9. Clusters, fourths and USTs work well when mixed together—for example, a UST on top of a voicing in fourths, or a section of music that alternates between these types of voicings.

Example 4.30 provides a variety of UST voicings.

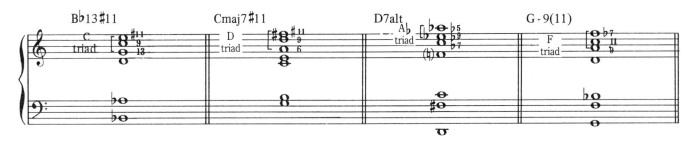

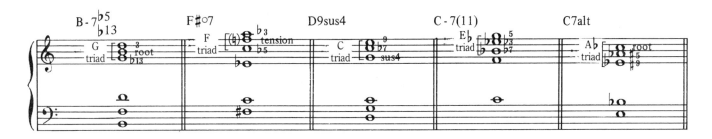

Upper-structure triad voicings used as ending chords

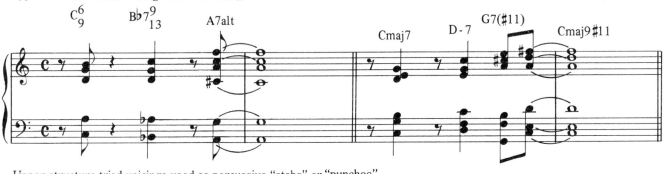

Upper-structure triad voicings used as percussive "stabs" or "punches"

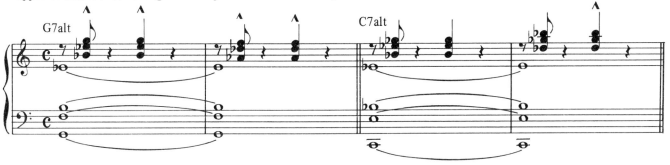

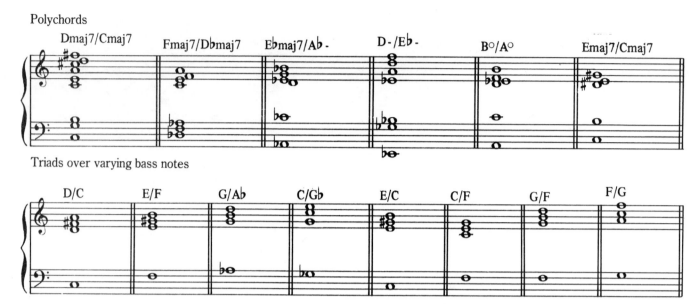

Example 4.30: *Various upper-structure triad voicings*

Polychords and Triads Over Bass Notes

A *polychord* is made up of two or more triads or chords from unrelated keys that are sounded simultaneously. Polychords are not one chord over various bass notes but are two distinct chord voicings from separate tonalities.

Triads over varying bass notes are triads placed over either diatonic or nondiatonic bass notes. This is an effective way to create harmonic tension within a key or by implying another key. These structures are effective in extensive reharmonization of a melody or for adding tension when the harmony moves slowly or

becomes too predictable. These techniques really stand out in an arrangement; it's hard to slip them in quickly. You are often dealing with more harmonic tension than usual, and the listener's ear needs time to assimilate the new sounds. Style and context will help determine when to use these techniques. A melody note will often indicate harmonic possibilities that are beyond the key of the moment. For example, a melody in the key of C could be thought of as the notes of a D♭7(alt) chord or as the notes of a nondiatonic triad. This technique can radically alter the sound and feeling of a melody. Example 4.31 provides various types of polychords and triadic reharmonizations and their applications.

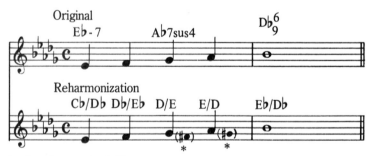

*note enharmonic spelling

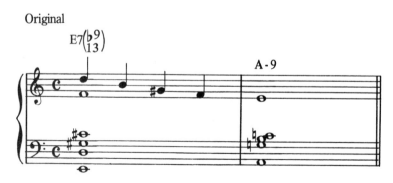

Example 4.31: *Polychords and triads over varying bass notes*

Reharmonization

This reharmonization makes use of what could be considered USTs of the original E7 voicing. Note the symetric pattern of descending minor thirds outlining an F°7 chord.

Original

Reharmonization

This reharmonization uses constant-structure major triads over bass notes which also follow the shape of the melody.

Example 4.31 *(continued)*

Unisons

Sometimes the most sensible thing to do, even in light of all the voicing options, is to write a unison. A unison or octave doubling is often the most dramatic tool. When in doubt, try a unison combination. A melody or background line can be best enhanced by doubling it at the unison or at some octave combination with complementary or contrasting sounds. A few distinct sounds played in unison are sometimes more powerful than the richest voicing.

Voiced passages are most effective when contrasted with a unison. Don't think of unisons as less desirable or last options because they are so "easy." In fact it's often easier to hide behind "hip" voicings than it is to construct a solid counterline or write unisons. Writing effective unisons is one of the hardest skills to master because they are so exposed.

Unisons have to be strong because there is nowhere to hide. Consider unisons as powerful options, not last-ditch alternatives.

Unison background writing can be so strong that it implies all the harmony you need to hear the chord progression. As an exercise, try writing strong unison lines to outline the harmonies of a song. See if you can really hear the chord progression with just the unison lines. Use your sequencer first to enter a melody, then enter the chord progression, and then write a unison background. Use separate tracks and MIDI channels. Play the melody and unison lines back, but mute the chord pad. Can you hear the chord progression? Are the implications contained in your unison lines? Try various sound combinations on the unisons. (See Example 4.32.)

Example 4.32: *Melody with unison-line background*

Extended Reharmonization

The purpose of reharmonization is to increase the possibilities for motion in places where the chord progression is basically static. *Extended reharmonization* involves major harmonic alterations to larger sections of an arrangement larger than just a few beats or measures. Reharmonization creates an increase in tension between the melody and the chords. Existing melody notes become higher tensions in the new chords. The following list of suggestions should help you plan your reharmonizations.

1. Determine what section of the song or piece needs reharmonization and why. How extensive should it be? How much tension do you want to create by changing the relationship of the melody to the chords? Before getting down to specific techniques, try to develop a general plan and reason for this procedure. In pop music you will often find that reharmonization occurs for only a few beats or bars at at time—often at ends of phrases, turnarounds, or when the melody is resting. Extended reharmonization often takes place in instrumental sections or when the singer has strong enough ears to not be confused by the new harmonic tension under the melody.

2. Find the most important target chords in the section. They often will be at beginning and ends of phrases. You may eventually change them, but initially you will use them as guideposts to work toward or from.

3. Analyze the melody, chord progression and phrase structure completely. Look for the obvious possibilities and implications for reharmonization. At first this will be a slow procedure, but with practice it can be done almost at a glance.

4. Write back from these target chords using a progression that produces a strong bass line. Again, writing back from your destination allows you to build toward a known chord. With practice you will be able to work toward the targets.

5. Determine which melody note(s) (if not all) will be reharmonized and choose the chords that fit them. The new chords need to relate to each other. You are building a new chord progression, not just individual chords for isolated notes. The combinations of chords must relate to each other and to the melody.

6. Choose chords whose roots will build a strong bass line. Try having the roots move in contrary motion to the melody, or try motion that at least does not parallel the melody.

7. Choose chords that have an increasingly rich relationship to the melody. (Melody notes become higher degrees of tension.)

8. Try writing a bass line first, moving in relative contrary motion to the melody, and then develop the types of chords. Fill in the inner voices last.

9. The guidelines for smooth voice leading apply here. The reharmonization itself will attract the listener's attention, so avoid distracting leaps or skips in the new inner voices.

10. Don't feel obligated to use every trick or technique you know in one section or piece. These are powerful techniques, so don't overuse them. A small amount of well-placed reharmonization can give new life to a static chord progression.

11. Be very conscious of tempo. Full, rich voicings, one after another, take time to have an impact on the listener's ear. Remember that these voicings have to work at the real tempo. You can spend hours piecing together a new chord progression

only to find that it's a blur at the real tempo. Each new voicing should be heard clearly; the faster the tempo, the less dense your voicings should be. This is one reason why unisons are so effective for relatively fast tempos. Use a sequencer and relate the reharmonization to the actual tempo.

There are two final points about reharmonization: (1) whatever technique you use, it must work with the melody and (2) there often are sections of an arrangement that involve harmony without melody. (The melody can be resting.) If this is the case, the techniques and voicings no longer have to support the melody, so you are free to explore other possibilities or implications.

There are many techniques and voicing types that can be combined for purposes of reharmonization. The following are among the most common.

1. *Tonic-Dominant Reharmonization.* Analyze the chord progression to determine if it is basically diatonic. If this is the case, you can define all the chords (except IV*) as being either tonic (containing two notes from the I chord) or dominant (containing two notes from the V or V7 chord). (See Example 4.33 for a tonic-dominant reharmonization.)

Tonic	Dominant
I, I6, Imaj7	V, V7
III –, III – 7	II –, II – 7
VI –, VI – 7	VII – 7(♭5)

The following are substitutions for the above chords:

Tonic Substitutions	Dominant Substitutions
♯IV – 7♭5	♭IImaj7, ♭II7, ♭II
III – 7♭5	♭VImaj7, ♭VI7, ♭VI – 7
I7	II7
V – 7	VII7
♭VI – 7	♭IIImaj7, ♭III7, ♭III – 7
♯IV7	

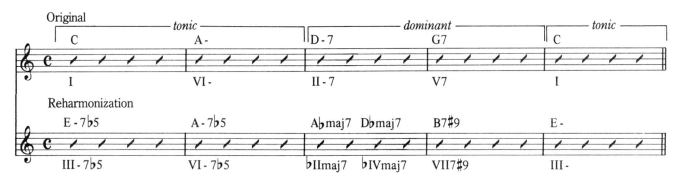

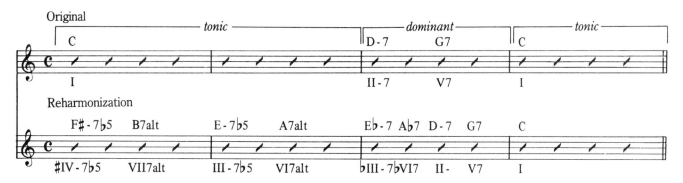

Example 4.33: *Tonic-dominant reharmonization*

2. *Reharmonization based on voice leading.* Chords can be altered so that the voices lead smoothly to alterations of the same chord or a new chord. You will need to alter the present chord so its top note moves smoothly to the next. (Example 4.34)

*IV can be a dominant, subdominant, or I chord in a new key. IV is a pivotal chord. Depending on the context or progression, it can have various functions.

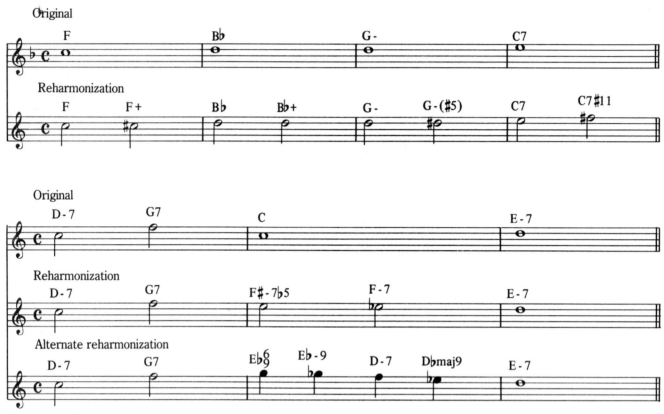

Example 4.34: *Reharmonization based on voice leading*

3. *Substitutions for passing diminished chords.* Most diminished chords can be replaced by related II – 7 ♭5 and V7(♭9) chords. The root of the related II – 7 ♭5 chord is usually found a minor third up from the diminished chord. The idea is that the II – 7 ♭5 and V7 ♭9 chords share common tones with the original diminished chord. You can think of this as the II – 7 ♭5 and V7 ♭9 of the chord to which the diminished chord was passing. Be sure to use this technique when the melody permits. The melody must contain chord tones or available tensions of the substitute chords. (See Example 4.35.)

Example 4.35: *Passing diminished-chord substitutions*

Example 4.35 (continued)

Additional diatonic-related substitutions. A diatonic substitution contains two common tones with the original chord, or at least one common tone is found in the melody. (See Example 4.36.)

Example 4.36: *Diatonic chord substitutions*

Example 4.36 (continued)

Tritone substitution. A dominant chord contains a tritone, comprising the third and seventh of the chord. The tritone (in Western music) divides the octave in half. This is the key to tritone substitution. Dominant seventh chords a tritone apart share identical tritones. The third and seventh of a G7 chord are the seventh and third of a D♭7 chord. A V7 chord, built on a root a tritone away, can be substituted for an existing V7

chord. The altered tensions of one are the natural tensions of the V7 chord a tritone away, and vice versa. This type of substitute for a dominant seventh chord is called a *subV*. You can also put the related II − 7 in front of a subV. This chord is a minor seventh chord a tritone away from the true II − 7, and so it is called a *subII*. (See Example 4.37.)

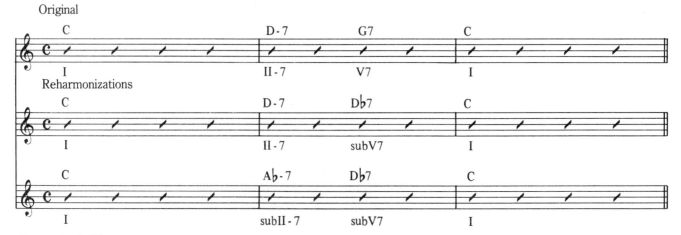

Example 4.37

You can extend this chain backward by using the V7 or subV of the subII and its related II− or subII, or by using a II V change based on the V or subV of subV. Examine the relationships among the substitute chords in each progression outlined in Example 4.38 to get an idea of how extensively this type of substitution may be used.

Example 4.38

Constant Structures

Constant structures are very useful in reharmonization. Constant-structure substitution is a mechanical technique that is imposed on a melody. You can think of any voicing by structure (spreads, fourths, clusters) or by function (major, minor). In constant-structure voicings decide what type of voicings (structures) to use for the section being reharmonized and then use that voicing (structure) on all the chords in the section. Table 4.7 and Example 4.39 illustrate the possibilities.

TABLE 4.7.

Possibilities for Constant-Structure Voicings.

Structure	Function
[1]Constant	Constant
[2]Constant	Variable
[3]Variable	Constant
[4]Variable	Variable

Note:

(1) Voicing structure of the same type (fourths, clusters, and so forth). Chord function remains the same (major, minor). For example, C−9, D−9, A−9. All use the exact same type of voicing, often in parallel motion.

(2) Voicing structures of same type; chord functions vary. For example, C−9, Bmaj7, D−9, A7; but all are voiced in fourths.

(3) Voicing structures vary, but chord types are the same. For example, C−9, D−9, E−9, F −9 voiced in a variety of ways (mixture of clusters, fourths, or spreads).

(4) Types of voicings and chords vary. For example, B −9, E 7 A maj9, F7(9) voiced in variety of ways, with a variety of structures.

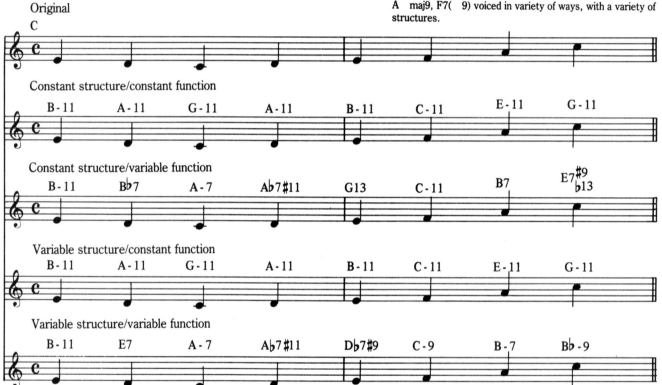

Example 4.39: Possibilities for constant-structure voicings

Here are a couple of interesting suggestions to open harmonic possibilities with constant structures. Assign each melody note a function or pattern of functions. For example, each melody note becomes an eleventh; or each melody note becomes (in order) a sharp-ninth, fifth, thirteenth, eleventh, sharp-ninth, fifth, thirteenth, eleventh. Repeat this pattern throughout the reharmonization section.

Here is a different approach. Set up a pattern that takes more or less beats to complete one measure. The pattern in Example 4.40 is five notes long, at one note per beat.

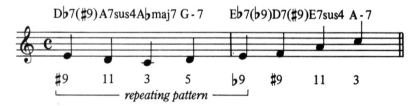

Example 4.40: Arbitrary pattern (♯9 11 3 5 ♭9)

You could also use this pattern as five eighth notes, so that it took less than one measure to complete. From this you can see the possibilities with which to experiment. If the technique seems arbitrary or clinical, it is; but that's not the point. Not every arrangement will warrant this treatment, nor will you use it extensively. The point is to experiment within a set or within arbitrary guidelines as a way of revealing possibilities that don't always appear immediately. It's like doing push-ups. By themselves they mean almost nothing, but if you can relate them to a larger context they somehow become more bearable. The goal is to explore harmonic possibilities and get your creative juices flowing by deliberately trying approaches that have not become your comfortable clichés. If you try this and it just doesn't work, you will still come back to the arrangement with at least one new idea. It will have been worth the effort.

By working with this technique you will also be able to envision harmonic possibilities or alternatives quickly. Having seen how many ways one note can function, you can handle reharmonizations quickly, logically, and with a bigger harmonic vocabulary.

Example 4.41 provides examples of extended reharmonization using combinations of techniques.

Example 4.41: *Extended reharmonization using combinations of techniques*

"Like Someone in Love"

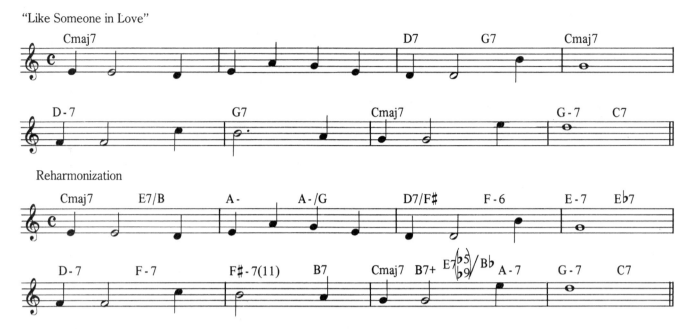

Example 4.41 (continued)

Pedal Point

A *pedal point* is a single note heard through a section of music. It may have sustained tones or rhythmically active tones. If active, it is a repetition of the same note with occasional other notes.

Pedal points usually appear in bass parts but may also occur in the middle or upper voices. They can also alternate between registers. Pedal points may make octave changes or adjustments. (For example, a single bass note may skip up and down octaves.)

While usually based around a tonic or dominant harmony, pedal points are commonly used as (1) *intros,* often where a theme or motif is stated over the pedal point; (2) *modulations,* chords heard over a sustained or active bass note, leading toward a new key; (3) *interludes,* important harmonic or melodic material heard against the pedal providing contrast to the rest of the arrangement; or (4) *thematic material,* stated against the pedal to build tension or contrast.

Example 4.42 illustrates common uses for pedal points.

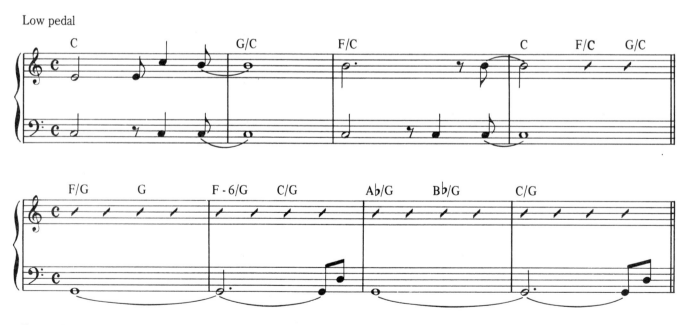

Example 4.42

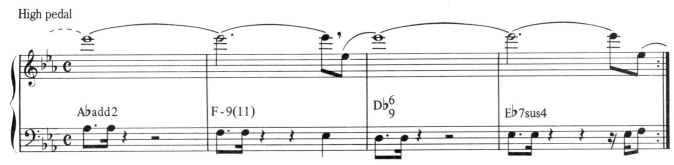

Example 4.42 *(continued)*

Ostinato

An *ostinato* is similar to a pedal point except that an ostinato involves a group of notes rather than one or two. Ostinati are usually melodic motifs that repeat over and over again in any register. For example, an ostinato bass line has a similar function to a low pedal, except that the ostinato has more notes, is more melodic, and is built in phrases rather than in single sustained or repeating notes. Michael Jackson's "Thriller" contains an ostinato bass line. Ostinati are heard in lots of sequencer based music. Both ostinati and pedals create tension harmonically and melodically.

Ostinati and pedals have similar emotional and musical effects. They are either single notes or repeating patterns that create tension in the harmony. The notes in both are derived from the chords or chord scales available. Analyze the chord progression, determine the chord scales, and select the appropriate notes to construct a pedal point or ostinato.

Example 4.43 gives common examples of ostinati.

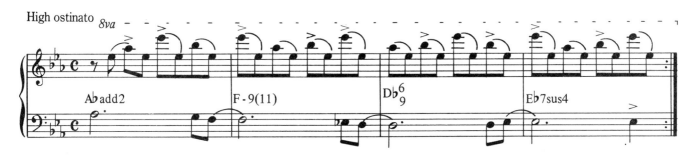

Example 4.43

Chapter Five
Strings

General Information About Acoustic Instruments

Understanding how to write for and program acoustic sounds on keyboards involves (1) knowledge of how acoustic instruments produce sound and the basic characteristics of these instruments, and (2) writing parts for these sounds. Acoustic sounds are incredibly popular on keyboards, and it's well worth the effort to become familiar with the nature of acoustic instruments, regardless of whether you have access to them or not. Your acoustic programs, samples, and parts are as authentic as your knowledge is complete. A great deal is known about acoustic instruments, and by infusing some of this knowledge into sounds, you can create better parts, samples, and patches.

Arrangers deal with the physical properties of sounds and develop musical parts for those sounds. The focus of this book is on music, not programming. For those of you who want an in-depth guide as to how to coax realistic acoustic sounds from your keyboards, I strongly recommend the book *A Synthesist's Guide to Acoustic Instruments,* by Howard Massey. It is the definitive technical guide to developing realistic acoustic sounds for keyboards. The book is full of timeless as well as up-to-date information on sampling, programming, acoustics, and sound design.

Not everyone has a full complement of acoustic musicians waiting to play through their next arrangement. Current technology provides an opportunity to improve your skills in areas that are necessary to becoming a competent arranger. Understanding acoustic instruments gives you a solid base for writing parts. Here are some general suggestions regarding writing for acoustic instruments and their keyboard equivalents.

1. Do a lot of analytical listening and transcribing. Practice separating the sound from the content (part). Listen to different elements of the sound; focus separately on timbre, register, the envelope (attack, decay, sustain, release—ADSR), articulation, phrasing, dynamics, and effects. For example, strings sound different in various registers or when plucked, bowed, or used in groups and solo.

2. Listen to the part, the musical content regardless of the sound. For example, the string part may be very well written, but the sound may be thin or brittle or the attacks may be too sluggish for the part. Listening to sound and content separately teaches you to develop your ears; to help you make critical judgements about what is effective (or not) and why; and to better understand the concept behind what you hear. This allows you to master the technique, not just imitate blindly.

3. If you are a keyboard-based arranger, you need to think like the player of the instruments for which you write. In reality, you are often the composer, arranger, and performer. This is very different than in the recent past, when arrangers had more contact with, and got lots of valuable suggestions from, the acoustic musicians who played what they wrote. Hang out with acoustic musicians of all styles. Pick their brains for suggestions on effective writing. Find out what works best in a given situation and why. What are their favorite records and why? Ask them to describe memorable moments in music that were either good or bad. In the same way that great synth programmers have special techniques for developing superb patches, acoustic players can offer equally valuable information that you can use, especially if you are writing acoustic parts using synths and samples.

4. Listen for the breathing spaces and phrasing in the parts. Synth-sampled strings will not physically tire if they don't rest or breathe, but your listeners will certainly get uncomfortable (even if they don't know why) when your parts don't breathe.

5. Current pop records often use a combination of synths and samples to make a composite acoustic instrument sound. In addition, these sounds are often blended with live musicians. In listening to the sound, try to figure out how it was developed. You may never know completely, but that's really not the point. You will have learned about sounds and writing in the process. A good exercise is to transcribe the string parts on a record and figure out as much as you can about the origin and nature of the sounds and the concept behind the parts.

6. String writing has not changed much, but the instruments have. The listening list at the end of this chapter covers a wide variety of styles and periods. In addition to using Howard Massey's book, study scores and records by twentieth-century composers. It helps to mark the scores with a highlighter pen as you listen.

Go to as many concerts and rehearsals as you can. Bring your scores and follow them carefully. Become familiar with the sounds and parts. If the situation permits, ask the players questions. Local or college chamber groups and orchestras will usually allow you to observe rehearsals free. Rehearsals are often more interesting than performances. You can hear the music several times and can watch the obvious and subtle difficulties get ironed out. You can even schedule a few private lessons with string players so that you can observe closely and ask questions.

The Acoustic Strings

Example 5.1 presents the members of the string family and their ranges, transpositions, and characteristics.

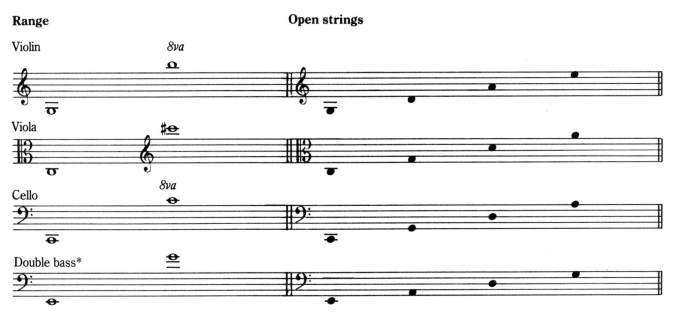

*Sounds one octave lower than written

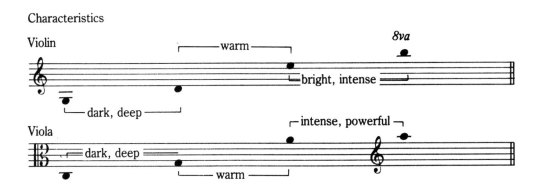

Example 5.1: *The string family*

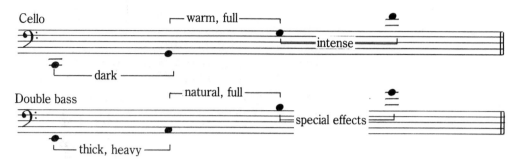

Example 5.1 *(continued)*

VIOLINS

The violin has the highest range of all the instruments in the string family.

The extreme high notes are not often used for commercial arrangements; the lower high register is used. The extreme high notes are best suited for solo passages.

The violin's tone quality is even and clear throughout the entire range. Each of the four strings has is own character, with the two inside strings being most similar. The top string (E) is bright and clear. The bottom string (G) is rich and warm.

Violins are perfect for background parts due to their neutral or transparent nature from midregister to the low end of the high register. Their potential to be soft and transparent allows them to be used for long periods of time without becoming tiresome to the ears (assuming the part is good).

When writing for violins, and strings in general, allow players time to change from pizzicato (plucked) to bowed sounds. Rapid leaps from high to low registers should always be a factor of tempo. Mix bowings and articulations to avoid monotony in your parts. Translating this into keyboard terms may mean using different patches for a part that has many characteristics, or it may mean selecting a patch or MIDI combination of patches that offers a reasonable compromise so you don't have to switch patches every time the parts vary.

If your collection of synth-sampled strings have long, sustained, slow-attack sounds, this limited supply of sounds will strongly influence your writing. Develop string sounds that have a wide variety of characteristics. We have all been guilty of writing string pads of long, slow moving parts because we didn't have sounds that could do otherwise. Such a part is sometimes perfect, but don't forget how versatile and dynamic strings can be.

VIOLAS

The viola is traditionally written in the alto clef, which places middle C on the middle line. Synth-string lines are usually written in the two-staff treble and bass system, and we tend to think of synth-strings as one general sound ranging from low to high. This is also a result of the sound usually being played from one keyboard. At first it's hard to think and write like a string player when you are sitting behind a keyboard. Even if most of us write string parts (when we write them at all) on one or two staves, it's important to know the differences between instruments.

The viola has the versatility of a violin, but it has a mellower sound due to its slightly larger size. The sound will not quite match the intensity of a violin, and it generally responds a little more slowly. The low C string has a thick, gritty character; the high A string is very warm and expressive.

When writing mid-to-high string parts, we often use the powerful combination of violins and violas in octaves. Try combining violin and viola solo or group patches in unison or octaves.

Group string sounds will always be thicker and richer than solo patches. The group sound has the natural, subtle, detuned sound of a group of instruments playing together. Any time you get a group of people playing the same note on the same type of instrument (even if they all play in tune) you still get some natural detuning due to individual differences in instruments, your position in the room, complex phasing, and resonance characteristics. The result can be a rich, warm sound. A group of violins will always sound richer than one person overdubbing the same note many times.

When writing string parts, determine whether you need group or individual sounds. Using a group sound and adding a solo patch on the top note can give extra clarity to active lines.

CELLOS

There are certain natural limitations to the possibilities of the cello. It can play rapidly, but not as rapidly as the violin or viola. It can play chords but they tend to blur when surrounded by other instruments in the same range. The first octave of the high A string is very expressive and rich, especially for lyrical melodies. The high extremes present serious intonation problems. The cello can do the same bowing, articulations, and harmonics of the higher string instruments, but it requires heavier finger pressure due to its thicker strings. The bow is shorter, thicker, and has a slower action. The strings are also higher off the neck. In general, the cello's response time is slower, but it can be used effectively for lyrical melodies in the higher register.

The cello's slower response time is why you should consider using patches that behave like a cello, in cello registers. This provides a very different sound than does playing a violin patch down three or more octaves.

Any acoustic instrument has natural limits to its range, but not so with a synthesizer patch. For example, a synth violin patch can easily be played in a register where it would never occur naturally. Very often what sounds false in synth strings is due to using the right patch in the wrong octave because you are not sure of the corresponding acoustic instrument's range. A good all-around synth string patch will have appropriate qualities from each string instrument.

DOUBLE BASS

The double bass is a transposing instrument and should be written an octave higher than it sounds. If you are writing for keyboard strings, write the notes as is. (Be sure to check the keyboard's octave transpositions.)

We often think of the double bass as being a pizzicato instrument because of its jazz role, but it has amazing expressive power when bowed. A section of bass is very powerful. Some interesting and unique sounds are available when the bass is bowed in the upper register. The bass often doubles the cello an octave below. In general, it responds slowly due to its size, string height, and thickness.

BOWING AND PHRASING

If a string part is written with the usual slurs, ties, and dots (to indicate legato or staccato), it will be played with a bow. If you want a part plucked (or pizzicato), write *pizz.* at the top of the staff where the change occurs. To switch back to bow, write *arco* where the switch is made.

On keyboards, these markings won't be literally translated, but they can help you make use of editing functions, after-touch, velocity sensitivity, use of sustain, and volume pedals. (See Example 5.2 for pizzicato and arco).

Example 5.2

When a bow is used, all the notes in one slur marking will be played in one bow direction, either up or down. The first slur in each measure or phrase will be played as a down-bow, unless otherwise indicated. Down-bows are marked with a ⊓ . Up-bows are marked with a ∨ . Bowing marks on a keyboard string part indicate how to phrase and where to place emphasis. This is one area where touch sensitivity and after-touch can add realism to the parts. The most natural pattern is to alternate between up- and down-bows (Example 5.3) Accomplished string players can change bow direction while sustaining a note with virtually no interruption. (This is not even an issue on keyboards, but don't let it become an excuse to sustain a note indefinitely.) Long sustained parts sound best (and more real) if they are reattacked, embellished or given some kind of subtle variation or dynamic. This gives a part some breath, or human feeling. (See Example 5.4.)

Example 5.3

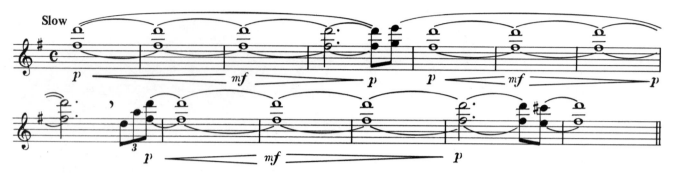

Example 5.4

Successive down-bows give a strong hammered effect, while successive up-bows give a lighter effect. Up-bows have a somewhat softer attack. Down-bows are heavier and louder and are normally used on accents and downbeats. (See Example 5.5.)

Example 5.5

Strings have traditionally had different types of staccato, or short notes. A dot over a note indicates staccato. This can be further clarified by an Italian description at the beginning of the section (for example, *spiccato*, rapid and light; *saltato*, jumping and bouncing; or *martelé*, hammered.

Dynamics are a function of the bow's pressure on the strings. The greater the pressure, the greater the volume. Dynamics are also relative, a fortissimo played on strings will not sound like a fortissimo played on a guitar with the amp set on stun. Some sounds are meant to be louder than others, yet keyboard strings can be as loud as you want. However, they sound best at levels that correspond to their acoustic relatives.

There are ways of creating the illusion of bigness or depth without resorting to volume. Some of this has to do with reverb settings, E.Q. panning, register, as well as well as the voicings. Avoid volume wars with string parts; create presence rather than sheer volume. Try doubling or thickening a part to create fullness. This way the strings can be big without becoming overbearing. Before doubling, either at the unison or in octaves, be sure you can justify the need. Make sure you aren't doubling a part that really needs to be rewritten or placed in another register. When written in the middle register string backgrounds have a more subdued presence than in high or low registers. In fact this is true for most background parts.

The following terms are frequently used in string writing, and although they are really designed for acoustic strings, becoming familiar with them will allow you to add more expressiveness and color to keyboard strings.

1. *Détaché.* Alternate bow direction with each note. String players use this when no other directions are given. The notes are separated by the change in bow direction (Example 5.6).

Example 5.6: *Détaché*

2. *Legato.* The curve mark over a group of notes indicates they are to be played in one bow direction. This is smoother than détaché) (Example 5.7).

Example 5.7: *Legato*

3. *Staccato.* Bow directions may or may not change (Example 5.8).

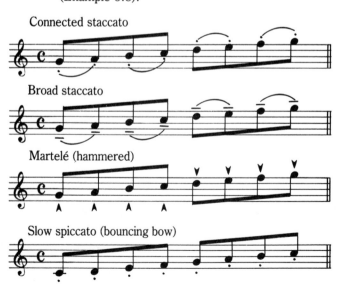

Example 5.8: *Types of staccato*

Example 5.8 *(continued)*

Fast spiccato

4. *Louré.* A type of legato bowing where a group of notes are played in one bow direction. This is very smooth (Example 5.9).

Example 5.9: *Louré*

5. *Tremolo.* Rapidly alternate up- and down-bows. This creates an exciting, bubbling effect. It can occur on the same note or alternating notes (Example 5.10).

Measured tremolo (on the same note)

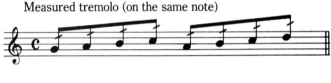

Fingered tremolo (trill between two notes)

Example 5.10: *Tremolo*

6. *Sul ponticello.* Play with the bow near the bridge. This creates a strident, edgier sound then the usual position midway between bridge and fingerboard. Write *sul ponticello* on the part where you want the bow change to occur.

7. *Sul tasto.* Play with the bow near or over the fingerboard. This gives a soft, warm sound.

8. *Punta d'arco.* Play the passage using only the tip of the bow. This is useful for soft, fast, and delicate passages where accuracy is critical. Mark the part accordingly.

9. *Col legno.* Turn the bow over and play on the wood. This creates a percussive, strident sound. Hitting the strings with the wood (*col legno battuto*) is even more percussive. This is similar to snapping the strings of an electric bass. However, acoustic string instruments can't take the heavy punishment like an electric bass, so use this sparingly.

10. *Glissando.* When two notes are played on one string, slide between them and the pitch will slide continuously also. Since there are no individual note increments as with the piano, the pitch bends in a continuous flow from note to note. This can be accomplished by using pitch bend on your synth (Example 5.11).

Example 5.11: *Glissando*

11. *Con sordino.* Play the string instrument with a mute. The mute is a small piece of wood or rubber that is clipped over the bridge. This produces a subdued, soft sound. Give the players time to place or remove the mute. With keyboards, a muted string sound can be achieved through programming and subtle E.Q. changes. *Senze sordino* means without a mute—back to normal.

12. *Ord.* (an abbreviation for *modo ordinario*). Cancel whatever special instructions were previously given and return to normal. On keyboards, this probably involves patch changes or modifications.

13. *Pizzicato (pizz.).* Pluck strings with the fingers. Keyboard pizz. strings are usually different patches or samples than sustained strings. In general, if your keyboard string parts use different string sounds, you may want to overdub a track of patch change information into your sequencer so that you don't get frustrated trying to switch patches and take the risk of cutting off notes. Try playing the string parts in real time and use no quantize (at least at first) for extra realism.

14. *Harmonics.* All acoustic strings have two types of harmonics, natural and artificial. *Natural harmonics* are produced by touching an open string lightly at spots (nodes) that are one-half, one-third, or one-fourth the length of the string. This produces the note at the corresponding position in the harmonic series (Example 5.12). *Artificial harmonics* are produced by placing one finger firmly down (at any spot) and another finger lightly (on the same string) a fourth or fifth above. Placing a finger a fourth above produces a tone two octaves higher. Placing a finger a fifth above produces a tone an octave plus a fifth higher (Example 5.13).

° = *natural harmonic*

Example 5.12: *Natural harmonics (on a cello's G string)*

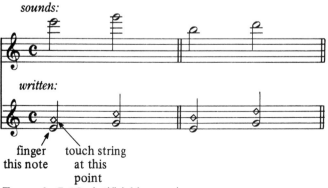

finger this note   touch string at this point

Example 5.13: *Artificial harmonics*

Natural harmonics are very strong and can be sustained. Artificial harmonics are more fragile, softer, and delicate. Simulating these effects on synthesizers requires some thoughtful programming, although very often another patch or a different register will imitate a harmonic sufficiently.

You can create samples of harmonics in the same way you sample a normally bowed note. Harmonics are very effective when used in higher registers and with ensemble sounds.

15. *Double stops* occur when two adjacent strings are played simultaneously. Fifths and sixths are relatively easy, as are consecutive or parallel fifths. Seconds, thirds, fourths, and augmented fourths are difficult unless the upper note is an open string. Octaves and sevenths that have an open string as a lower note are also easy. Double stops work best on cello and bass with open

strings sounding as much as possible. In general, players need time to adjust hand positions for double stops. You can occasionally get three-note chords by combining a double stop with a note from the next adjacent string. Sixths or fifths and sixths usually work well.

On keyboards the only fingering problems are those inherent to keyboards, and sequencing will overrule most fingering problems. Creating double stop sounds on keyboards is usually nothing more than playing the notes you wanted anyway. In the final analysis any string part written on keyboard may reach many ears, so try to make your parts sound believable to nonmusicians too. Double stops are often written for small string sections to get a small number of people to play more notes. Example 5.14 outlines available double stops for violin, and Example 5.15 shows how to transpose these for viola and cello.

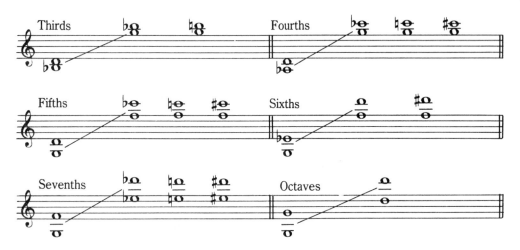

Seconds should be avoided unless an open-string note is used

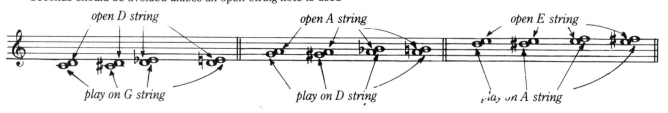

Example 5.14: *Double stops available on violin*

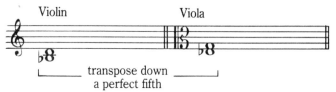

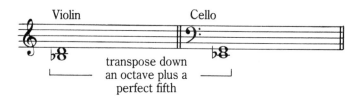

Example 5.15: *Double stops available on viola and cello*

DYNAMICS

As mentioned before, dynamics are relative, and strings (in relation to themselves) are capable of a wide dynamic range. The string instruments are very flexible and responsive to dynamic input. This is

something to remember and strive for in writing keyboard string parts. Dynamics should be considered an integral part of string writing, not an afterthought. Lack of dynamics can be compared to speaking in a monotone. It's not just what you say, but how you say it. It seems that we spend so much time programming and writing that dynamics get overlooked. Learn to use the functions of your instruments that allow for dynamic expression. Listen to the records on the listening list or get some other good classical, contemporary, or pop records that have strings.

Dynamics are often created by gradually adding or taking away instruments or by adding and removing doublings on a given line or part. This is very effective with strings. Adding or removing doublings of a unison, or doublings on notes in a voicing can create a kind of dynamics. It thickens and thins out the texture.

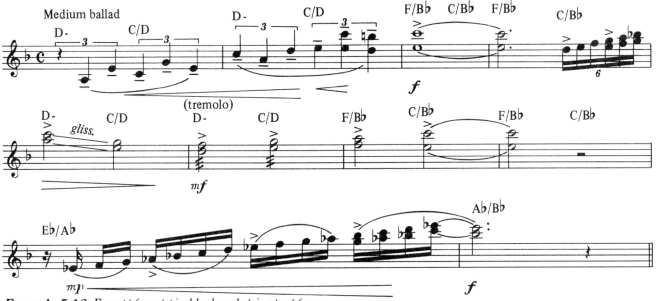

Example 5.16: *Excerpt from typical keyboard string part (use a combination of analog and digital synth patches and samples—ensemble-type sounds)*

VOICINGS

Acoustic instruments, particularly strings, are naturally rich in harmonics, and this is why there is an illusion of harmony even when they are played in unison. The harmonies you write become intensified by the naturally rich nature of the instruments. This is what we strive for in creating realistic synth string patches. A simple unison line played by a string ensemble patch has the illusion of being voiced. The implication here is that string voicings that are too thick can muddy the arrangement. Good string writing involves strong, clear linear parts with simple voicings, thirds, sixths, and unison or octave doublings. It is best to stay simple to begin with; you can always add more motes if you need to.

The rules for background writing mentioned earlier certainly apply to strings. The background becomes more active when the melody rests. Allow for sufficient contrast in sounds, registers, rhythmic activity, and dynamics.

On the piano, quick changes of register, chords, and voicings are physically easy and are clearly heard. The same rapid changes would be difficult to hear and would be less clear in a string ensemble. Due to the strings' rich nature, voicings should be simpler and move less rapidly than piano parts. Once again, this brings home the point about not assuming your keyboard voicings and parts will work on other sounds.

Practical Suggestions

1. Work on writing string countermelodies as opposed to "comping through the chords using a string sound." Develop parts that have melodic, harmonic, and rhythmic identities of their own and that are complete musical statements.

2. Write parts in different registers, or write parts that encompass several octaves. Learn to make decisions about the octave(s) in which a part is most effective.

3. Some arrangements will require only minimal string writing. For example, the string part may be no more than a high, soft, sustained line, way back in the mix. Practice objective evaluation of your work, and continuing experimentation will provide you with the wisdom to make effective musical decisions.

4. Consider where in the measure a line or note should enter. Should the part ease in or enter dramatically? Analyze the melody and anything else that's going on to determine the best place for your entrances. Choosing the right beat to enter on can give the part elegance, power, or subtlety.

5. Strings are best added to an arrangement when you are sure of what the melody or vocal is doing. In recording situations, plan the strings as an overdub so you can study what's already in place. For live performance, write the strings after you have worked out the details of the melody, vocals, and basic rhythm arrangements.

6. Ask yourself if the lines or parts are intrusive or supportive. Are they rhythmically complementary, or do they conflict with other elements? Would the part work better an octave below or an octave above? Is the sound too thick or too thin? Is the sound working well with the voicing?

7. Strings sound best if allowed to taper off naturally when they are finished playing. Leave yourself room to let the sound fade or sustain naturally (with the right notes) into the next section. Abrupt cutoffs only work with fast-attack, fast-decay sounds. Strings can be used percussively, but choose the right sounds. Holding the last note of a string line into the next section often solves the problem of how to make a transition. This technique alone can provide continuity in transitions.

8. Choose a pop or standard song with a strong melody and orchestrate it for a string section. Use your keyboard string sounds to make a string-section sound. Try this combination: three violins, one viola, one cello. Let the top violin play the melody note or have an inner part play the melody with the harmony surrounding it. Use any of the voicing types described earlier. Put the parts in your sequencer, line by line, on separate tracks or MIDI channels.

9. Try the following approaches:

(a) Have one instrument (patch) play the melody, while the background sustains (chorale style).

(b) Use as many bowing, phrasing, and articulation effects as you can (not necessarily on only one version) to hear how they sound in context.

(c) Try activating the under parts so they have their own identities. Use passing tones, and so forth.

(d) Try a contrapuntal version. Use the melody as the theme for a canon and develop it. The sequencer is very handy for this.

(e) Use pedal point or ostinato above or below the melody. Keep or alter the original harmony.

(f) Write a countermelody in addition to filling out the harmony.

(g) Write the melody for one string sound. Write a countermelody for another string sound. Have these two sounds make a complete statement, implying other notes in the harmony.

CHAPTER SIX ✍
ACOUSTIC BRASS

Modern brass instruments are the direct descendents of primitive hunting and battle horns. Much of that original urgency, intensity, and power is still there. It's no wonder that even in this era of great synth and sampled brass we still love hearing and watching live horn players. There is nothing like the urgency and power of a live horn section on a record or in performance. Loading a horn-section sample into the latest gear and hitting the right keys just doesn't feel the same for the players or the audience. People like to see and feel the interaction of live players. This is not meant to put down keyboard horns because there are many valid circumstances to obviate their value. At the least, not every arranger is surrounded by a great horn section or has the budget or mic's for one.

The great thing about modern brass instruments is that with all the mechanical improvements and modifications over their ancestors, they still can stir the soul. Brass instruments produce sounds by blowing into a length of tubing. The lips are the vibrating medium. Part of the "stuff" in brass patches and samples is the lip noise, and the saliva gurgling—the sound of human flesh being made to vibrate against metal.

Brass players absolutely need to breathe and rest between particularly difficult or high parts. It takes a lot of power and concentration to produce and control sound on brass instruments. Many a naive keyboard arranger has seen brass players' lips turn to hamburger after suffering through a needlessly overwritten arrangement. Players also need rests to allow the blood to return to their lips.

The value of acoustic instruments on a synth-sample based record is immediately apparent. The acoustic sounds become fresh once again in their new contexts, and the electronic sounds are given a different perspective and warmth. The two traditions can musically coexist if we allow each to do what it

does best. Arif Mardin, one of the world's greatest arranger-producers is a master at combining leading-edge, hi-tech sounds and acoustic instruments into brilliant and coherent arrangements. When acoustic and electronic sounds and parts are blended well, the whole is greater than the sum of the parts.

Brass sounds can be divided into three categories:

1. *Warm:* French horn

2. *Dark or Mellow:* tuba, sousaphone, baritone horn, clarinet, flügelhorn

3. *Clear-bright:* trumpet, trombone (which can really function in all three categories).

General Suggestions

Rimski-Korsakov made some interesting observations in his book on orchestration. He said, "The more intense a sound or texture is, the less you can endure it over a period of time." This explains why we hear more of some sounds than others. Rimski-Korsakov also said that the most intense sounds were percussion and bells, followed by the brass and woodwinds. Least intense were the strings, which can be used for the longest time without becoming annoying.

Brass instruments can also be used for longer passages—more often in middle registers than extremes. Any type of control, finesse, and endurance becomes more difficult when playing in extreme registers. Yet brass, especially trumpets and trombones, are really exciting in the high registers. Give your players a chance to rest before and after a difficult high part. Also, it's physically much easier to play in the upper extremes when the under parts are well written, the voicings are balanced, and the other higher notes closely support the top notes. Well-balanced voicings are as important from a performance standpoint as they are in writing. The assignment of sounds to notes of a chord (or unison) should take into account their inherent strengths and weaknesses. For example, it takes two French horns playing mezzo forte to balance one trumpet or trombone at the same volume. You must adjust the dynamics to fit the available instrumentation if the situation is not ideal. This is relatively easy in recording, especially on consoles with lots of inputs, but it's best to know about these tendencies so you can anticipate problems. Big gaps in the voicings are not only musically ineffective but are also physically disturbing to players. Well-balanced voicings help players keep strong pitch and blend reference. Lead players especially need strong physical support in the under parts.

A brass section, or any horn section, needs players (or patches) whose sounds blend and who have similar physical endurance (not a problem for keyboards). Getting a blend or balance is dependent on three things: (1) that the parts are well-written and the voicings are balanced from the start; (2) that the players or patches blend or complement each other; and (3) that the right attitude exists for live players to produce a blend. The players must want to blend; it's teamwork, and the lead player is the captain. The best horn sections are those where each person leaves his or her ego at the door and plays for the music, not for individual attention. When they work at and achieve a rich blend, everyone wins.

Good pitch is as much a matter of attitude and cooperation as it is a matter of absolute values. Brass instruments, like all acoustic instruments, do not automatically play in tune. Players must constantly make fine adjustments to themselves and other players. With keyboards it is much easier; you can change or edit discs and patches until you get what you want or what seems reasonable for lack of live players. It is becoming common practice today to have a mixture of live horns and keyboard horns playing the same or complementary parts.

Using a brass sample or patch that is loud will sound best used just that way. For example, a sample of a high, loud trumpet note will sound unnatural if mixed or played too low. It makes more sense to get a sound that really fits your needs. Brass players move a lot of air by playing loudly, and it sounds unmusical when a sample is used at too low a volume in a mix or performance. Conversely, a sample taken at low volume, in mid-register, will lack the natural intensity if replayed too loud or high. It will sound like the player is somehow able to play the note without the necessary energy to do so.

Most samples have a limited range of effectiveness. A sample is taken on a given note, in a certain register. Moving too far away from that original place makes it sound peculiar due to the arbitrary change in natural harmonics that occurs.

Mutes make a big difference in the sound and dynamic power of brass instruments. There are a wide variety of mutes for brass, each of which has a characteristic sound. Some of the most common are cup, bucket, plunger, and harmon (with or without the stem). Mutes reduce volume, change sound, and somewhat inhibit the range. The best way to become familiar with mutes is to spend time with brass players, listening and asking questions, attending rehearsals, and concerts, reading scores while listening, and checking the listening list that appears at the back of this book.

Brass instruments have an enormous potential for dynamic range. Except in extreme registers, they can go from pianissimo to fortissimo easily and are effective with markings like forte-piano, sforzando, and sudden crescendos and diminuendos. Quick changes from extremely high and loud to low and soft are not practical. On keyboards this is not a problem, but it will sound very unnatural and more like a special effect.

Acoustic brass are basically an interconnected series of metal tubes, valves, and slides. Each length of tubing has its own strong, resonant quality and fundamental tone in the harmonic series. Players open and close valves or move slides to choose notes in the harmonic series that are available from a given fundamental. This is done with varying amounts of air pressure and lip vibrations.

Example 6.1 presents is a list of acoustic brass, their ranges, and their transpositions.

Example 6.1: *Brass ranges and transpositions (○=full range,*
●= useful, practical range)

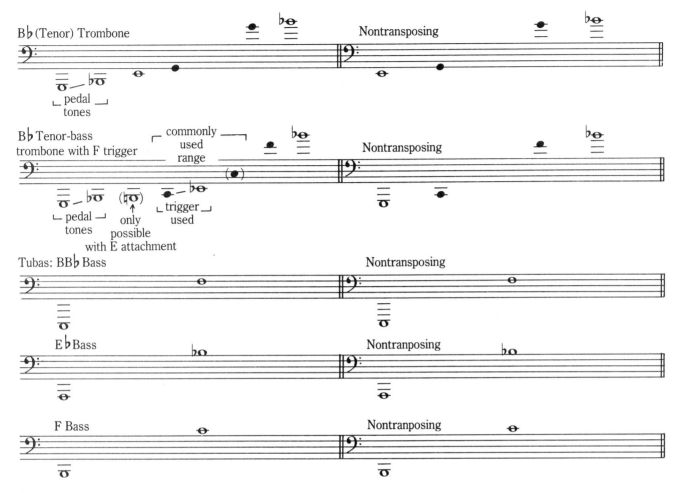

Example 6.1 *(continued)*

Trumpets

There are three types of trumpets in general use. Synth and sampled trumpet sounds usually start out with these instruments as a reference.

1. *Standard B-flat trumpet.* This is by far the most common of the trumpets, with a clear sound and wide range. It is a transposing instrument, and its part must be transposed up a major second from concert pitch. For example, middle C would be written for trumpets as D, a major second higher.

2. *B-flat cornet.* This is a close relative of the trumpet but has a mellower sound due to the different bell and bore. It has the same transposition as the trumpet but less overall edge.

3. *Flügelhorn.* This is a larger-bore, larger bell version of the trumpet with a very warm, rich, fat sound in all registers. Due to the larger bore, the sound has less edge, and the upper register doesn't extend as far as that of the trumpet. The lower register is richer than the trumpet's, again due to the large bore. The flügelhorn blends well with all the brass and most other timbres. It's often used as a solo instrument because of its warm, pleasing sound, and it is very popular in jazz. The flügelhorn's sound is ideal for soft passages. It has the same transposition as the trumpet. (Freddie Hubbard and Chuck Mangione use flügelhorn extensively.)

Trumpets, cornets, and flügelhorns are often played with devices called *mutes* placed in their bells. The different types of mutes change the timbre of the instrument, making it thinner and softer, less strident. However, mutes also limit the effective range of the instrument, as shown in Example 6.2.

Example 6.2: Effective ranges of muted trumpet (as written)

French Horn

The French horn is a transposing instrument that sounds a perfect fifth lower than it is written. It has a very wide range, but in actual practice the most useful notes are limited to an octave and a fifth. The notes in the extremes are somewhat difficult to play and present some pitch problems. Extreme high notes sound tense, and extreme low notes should only be used for special effects.

The French horn is often played with a hand inserted in its bell. This places the instrument a half step higher than when the bell is open. However, there is no additional transposition needed; the players make the adjustments. These muted, or *stopped,* notes are indicated by a plus sign (+) above them.

The tone of the French horn is flexible and expressive. Players can put a lot of character (gurgle, buzz, roughness) into its sound. When a mute is inserted, the sound becomes mysterious and distant. The modern French horn is capable of a wide dynamic range and is quite flexible in playing parts within the useful range. Legato sections must allow for breathing room, and staccato sections should not be too fast or long without rests.

The mouthpiece is small, requiring substantial pressure and concentration, so entrances and articulations should be given consideration (that is, give the players enough time to prepare and breathe between difficult sections.)

Since the French horn does not skip easily between registers, write parts with smooth voice leading, and stay within the same range for a given phrase. (See Example 6.3.)

Example 6.3

Trombone

The standard trombone is the B-flat or tenor trombone, and the tenor-bass or bass trombone in F is also common. Trombones are nontransposing, with the parts written exactly as they sound. The natural harmonics of the instrument are the most easily played notes.

As the trombone's slide is extended, lower notes are played. Below each naturally occurring harmonic, a series of half steps occurs, and they correlate to one of the seven positions on the slide. (See Example 6.4.)

Example 6.4: *Some trombone slide positions*

The notes closest to the harmonic that require the least movement of the slide are easiest to play. Parts are easiest to play when the slide is moving gradually. The instrument is so flexible in tone quality, range, and expressiveness that it can be used in many ways. In small horn sections, high trombone parts sound well mixed in with trumpet parts. Be sure to know a player's strength in the upper register or keep the top note below A, a sixth above middle C. The trombone sounds great in unison or octave doublings with brass, or mixed reed-brass sections. In using trombone samples, it will sound best used close to the note at which it was originally sampled.

Pure legato is a little tricky due to the shifting of slide positions, but good players will not have trouble playing smooth, connected passages without reattacking notes. Staccato articulations on trombone are slightly less crisp than on the trumpet. *Glissando* (gliss.) should be limited to the six half steps below each harmonic; otherwise there will be a break in the glissando. Like the trumpet, the trombone is often played with one of several types of mute, and this affects its effective range. (See Example 6.5.)

Example 6.5: *Effective ranges of muted trombone*

Bass Trombone

Everything said about the tenor trombone applies to the bass trombone except that the bass trombone responds somewhat slower to input from the player. It is most effective use of bass trombone (unless you have virtuoso players) in the lower half of its range. Most players develop the ability to anticipate the slow response time in order to make the notes come out in time, rather than slightly delayed. The tenor-bass trombone, which is widely used, alleviates these problems through the use of an *F trigger* attachment for the lowest tones.

Tuba

The tuba is a nontransposing instrument, written as it sounds. There are several varieties of tuba. The B-flat baritone horn is the highest-pitched tuba; it corresponds to the tenor trombone, and is often used in place of it. The lowest-pitched tuba is the low B-flat (sometimes called the *double B-flat* or *BB-flat*). It is also called the Sousaphone. The low B-flat is more common in bands and marching bands and has a huge wraparound bell. The higher bass tubas in E-flat are more common in orchestral music because they are not so sluggish and have more available high register notes. It is best to avoid high- and low-register extremes unless you really know a player's abilities.

The tuba is most often used as the deep bottom of a brass section or orchestra but only when that depth and fullness is needed. The trombones often fill this role. Tubas are also known for their roles in traditional Dixieland music. Tubas are slow to respond to a player's input. Articulation and attacks are slow, and staccato is sluggish. There are a few virtuosos who have almost overcome the tuba's inherent problems, but don't count on it. Good players will have flexibility and control in the upper register, where the instrument can be warm and melodic.

Articulation, Special Effects

Since the brass are capable of a wide range of articulations and special effects (Example 6.6), well-marked parts are a must for live players and keyboard brass as well. The type of part you write (that is, staccato, legato, mixed) will influence your choice of synth patches or samples. Even if you are using keyboards, write out the parts on a condensed (double-stave) score. This helps you find problems with the part. Make sure there are enough rests and dynamics to make the part sound believable. You may even end up adding some live horns to your electronic horns, so be prepared with a score from which to copy the parts. The most realistic keyboard brass parts are those that don't rely heavily on special effects (trills, flutter tongue, valve slurs). These are difficult, if not impossible, on many samples or patches. Keep your keyboard horns straight ahead with a minimum of special effects.

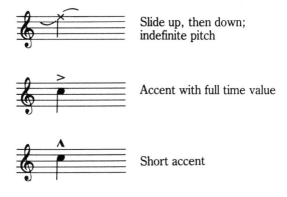

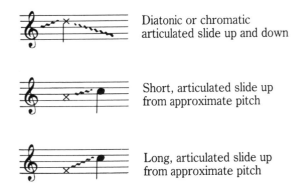

Example 6.6: *Brass articulations and special effects*

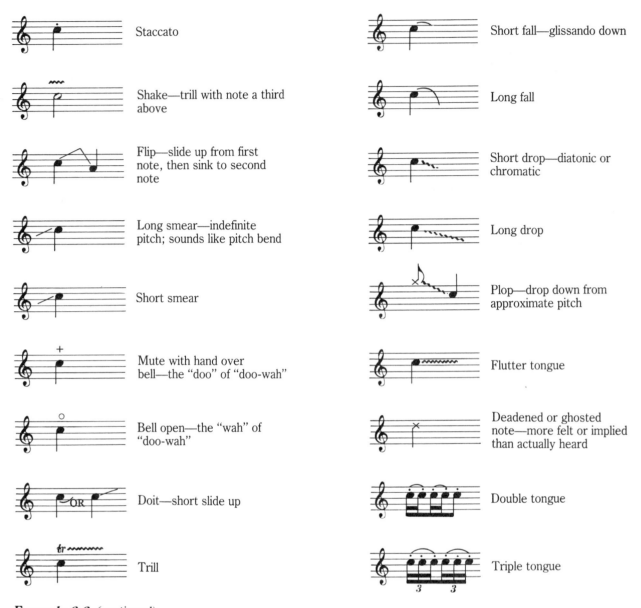

Example 6.6 *(continued)*

Additional Suggestions

1. The information supplied about voicings in the "Harmony" chapter also applies to brass. Brass sections can be voiced with any type of voicing. Remember to balance the voicing, no matter what type. Avoid large gaps and seconds between the top notes. You should generally have reasons for using a particular voicing or combination of voicings. (Chapter Eight—"Small Horn Sections"— will discuss typical voicings for mixed brass and saxes.)

2. The area of sampling is in the midst of heavy legal and ethical debate at this time. Follow the course of events in this area, as it will undoubtedly affect all of us. Discs you buy from reputable companies are probably clear of any litigation. Sampling someone's horn sounds from a compact disc and blatantly using them without permission may be an infringement of copyright, and thus you are at risk. It is done all the time, but that does not make it legal. If possible, make your own samples. This is the best way to learn about the process.

3. Try writing horn parts to a record that doesn't have any. Write active and sustained parts. Try different combinations of sounds in different registers. Write simple, short, punctuated parts or more involved counterlines.

4. Try any or all of the suggestions at the end of the Chapter Five ("Strings").

5. Write a brass ensemble version of a pop song. Write different versions varying the sound playing the melody.

6. Transcribe horn parts from records. Dissect the voicings and instrumentation. Write similar horn parts for another song.

7. Study printed scores for big bands, orchestras, jazz or pop groups, chamber groups, or brass ensembles.

CHAPTER SEVEN ✍
WOODWINDS

The original woodwinds had wood and metal pipes or reeds with holes drilled into them. Sound was produced by blowing across a hole bored into a pipe (for example, the flute) or by blowing into a whistle-like mouthpiece (for example, the recorder or whistle). James Galway has popularized the Irish pennywhistle, which is played this way. Sound can also be produced by blowing against a single reed causing it to vibrate against a solid surface attached to a wood or metal tube (for example, the saxophone or clarinet). A woodwind can also be played by blowing against two joined reeds that vibrate against each other and that are attached to a tube or pipe (for example, the oboe or bassoon).

The original woodwinds were badly out of tune by today's standards because the holes were unevenly spaced and hand positions were awkward. This situation was as good as it could be in an attempt to play in tune. If the holes were close together to make fingerings and hand positions comfortable, the intonation would have been much worse. In time a system of keys and levers were developed to create comfortable fingerings while allowing the holes to be placed at strategic places for good intonation. The modern Boehm system is named for the man who is largely responsible for modernizing woodwinds.

Relative perfection is fairly recent, within the last two hundred years and in some cases much less. These improvements, which began in the mid-nineteenth century, have allowed woodwinds to take on much greater musical importance. A quick look at scores by early classical composers shows woodwinds in restricted roles. There are records and occasional concerts of early classical music played on actual instruments (or replicas) of the period. Even with great players, the intonation is miserable. (Mozart and Bach must have pulled their hair out on more than one occasion.) It does give us an appreciation for advances in technology, however. No doubt there were people who resisted putting more keys on a clarinet, just as there are people who say that synthesizers are not real instruments. The debate will probably go on as long as people are willing to argue the point.

As woodwinds became technically more agile and their timbres more varied, they rose from restricted to featured roles. Debussy, Ravel, and Stravinsky did a great deal to bring woodwinds into the forefront of classical music. Dixieland, swing, and bebop also established new roles for woodwinds. Classical and jazz composers challenged players with music that fully utilized the technical potential of woodwinds. Some legendary works include Debussy's *La Mer* and *Iberia;* Stravinsky's *The Rite of Spring, Petrushka,* and *The Firebird;* and Ravel's *Daphnis and Chloé.* The music of Duke Ellington, Louis Armstrong, Artie Shaw, and Benny Goodman explored and challenged the technical abilities of woodwind players.

The extreme registers are the most difficult, but they are not impossible to control. Often the upper registers are the most passionate. The middle registers offer the widest range of flexibility, dynamics, and expression. The fullest and richest sounds are usually found in these registers. (The chart on articulations and effects in Chapter Six also applies to woodwinds.)

Woodwinds can play legato passages in one breath, the same way a singer does when singing a phrase. Legato passages should be marked to coincide with beginnings and ends of phrases where players would naturally breathe. (See Example 7.1.) Legato phrases can be played as long as a player can hold his or her breath. Staccato is effective and easy. It helps to add some additional instructions on parts, such as "short," "crisp," or "on top" (of the beat). It is also useful to indicate who else is playing the same or similar parts. This alerts players as to whom they should blend with or listen to for cues, pitch-references, phrasings, entrances, or cutoffs.

Example 7.1: *Legato phrasing*

Separate notes that are not legato are attacked-tongued with the syllable *tu* or *ta*. Double tonguing is done with *tu-ku* or with tongue and throat alternating. (Try saying these syllables to get an idea of how woodwind players articulate.) Alternating tongued and slurred or legato and staccato passages is relatively easy, except in extreme registers. Woodwinds are like human voices in their expressive power, so try singing the parts as you write them. If you can sing a part, it will probably be playable, if not musical. (See Example 7.2.)

Example 7.2: *Staccato and legato phrasing*

Flutes, clarinets and saxophones are very agile, but saxophones are slightly sluggish on staccato passages. This is due to the shapes of their bores, which are conical. (The diameter opens gradually like a cone.) The other woodwinds' bores are cylindrical. (The diameters are the same size from beginning to end.)

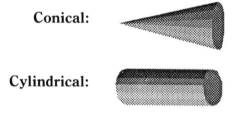

Conical:

Cylindrical:

The bassoon is moderately agile and is a natural for staccato passages. The oboe sounds best when there is a limited amount of staccato because of the tremendous physical concentration the oboe demands. It sounds best on lyrical, legato passages that have a moderate melodic range.

Bass clarinet and bassoon are usually known for their rich low-register qualities but they are very expressive in middle and upper registers. With good players the possibilities are extensive. If you are not sure of a player's abilities, write more conservatively. As mentioned in previous chapters, listen, transcribe, observe, and ask as many questions as you can.

One other observation about woodwinds is that in order for them to be heard to their full potential; they must either be in a brilliant register or the background must be fairly transparent. Woodwinds tend to get absorbed by a denser background. When they double string parts, the strings tend to absorb

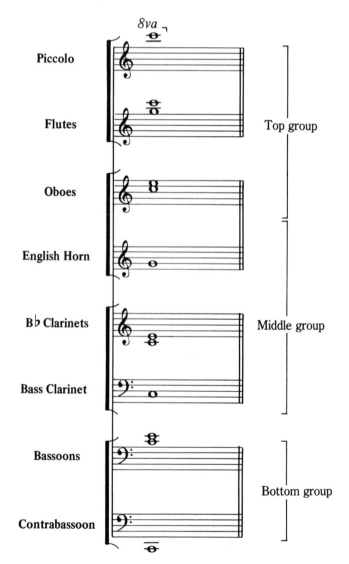

Example 7.3: *Distribution in woodwind voicings*

them, yet the overall texture becomes richer. This is not a negative observation. In fact, on keyboards you can blend these timbres to your advantage. Woodwinds enhance string sounds, as long as you follow the general guidelines for solid voicings. Also implied here is the fact that woodwinds stand out best when their parts are independent and active.

Woodwinds blend well with each other, particularly when you combine two of one group with one of another. (For example, two clarinets and one bassoon, two flutes and one oboe, or two bassoons and one bass clarinet. These groups of three play areas of voicings that often overlap. This adds warmth and color to a chord.) (See Example 7.3.)

The practical ranges in Example 7.4 are conservative. Accomplished players have no trouble playing the full range with good intonation and technique. (The comments and suggestions in the previous chapters also apply here.)

*only possible with low-B key

Example 7.4: *Woodwind ranges and transpositions (**o**= full range, **●** = useful, practical range)*

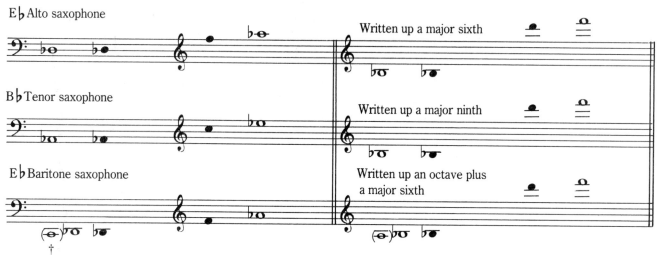

† only possible on low-A models

Example 7.4 *(continued)*

The Acoustic Woodwinds

PICCOLO

The piccolo sounds an octave higher than the flute. Its sound is unique and different from the flute. It can be very intense and brilliant in color. It is used most in its highest register, although the middle register is attractive. We are all familiar with Popeye and the classic cartoons and marches that used the piccolo in a comical way. The instrument can also be used without being shrill or comical. It is often used to double a flute part an octave higher or in exact unison. At the exact unison the piccolo sound is absorbed by the flute, but it adds a subtle color. The low register of the piccolo does not project as well as other registers,

but it is warm and expressive. These qualities won't be heard through any kind of thick texture.

The fingerings for the piccolo are the same as those for the flute, and many players are competent on both. There also is a piccolo in D-flat (very rare), and it's used in bands. It transposes down a minor ninth.

FLUTE

The flute sounds as written. It is extremely expressive and flexible over its entire range, although it is somewhat difficult to play loud in the lower register. Each of the flute's three octaves has its own characteristic sound. (See Example 7.5.)

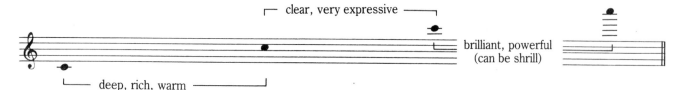

Example 7.5: *Characteristics of the flute sound*

The classic low-register flute sound can be heard in Debussy's *Afternoon of a Faun.* The lowest register does not project like the upper two registers, so be sure the surrounding texture is not so dense that the subtle qualities are lost. The middle register is clear, and a player with a rich, well-developed tone can give the middle register an illusion of sounding lower. The highest octave is brilliant and has inherent pitch problems that good players know about and are capable of correcting. The third octave is still very expressive and is often used to double other instruments. Fortissimo will be softer on the flute than

on the trumpet. As an arranger, you constantly need to be aware of the other sounds and dynamic levels. Even though the flute is small, it requires tremendous breath support and concentration. Give flute players chances to rest and relax their embouchures. The flute is natural for lyrical passages and any melodic playing. It also sounds well over string backgrounds.

If your flute parts have a wide range of articulation and dynamics, the keyboard version will require careful selection of patches, samples, and edits to accommodate the variety. Consider using your sequencer to handle the patch changes. If this seems clumsy or time-consuming, you can always write out the part and get an actual player. This is often the best solution, especially for parts with lots of character.

ALTO FLUTE IN G

The alto flute has the same written range as the C flute, but its parts transpose a perfect fourth higher. Its sound is incredibly warm and rich. It blends well with the C flute and with most other instruments. An alto flute sound can be used to double, thicken, or support many different sounds. Its most characteristic sound is in the two lower octaves. The third octave sounds like a thicker C flute.

The alto flute sounds well as a support for two C flutes in a flute group or blended with flügelhorn, French horn, or any warm synth sound. You can write

for alto flute the same way you write for C flute, but the response is a little slower due to its size. This is not a problem; in fact it's part of the instrument's uniqueness and beauty. It works very well on lyrical, expressive melodies.

OBOE

When the oboe is well played, it is one of the most expressive, intense, and passionate instruments. But it is one of the more difficult instruments to play well. The small bore and double reed combination require tremendous breath support and concentration. It's best to keep parts in the middle register since the high and low registers are extremely hard to control except in the hands of accomplished players. Simple legato passages with occasional well-prepared leaps sound best. (See Example 7.6.)

Example 7.6: Typical "safe" writing for oboe parts

Allow for breathing space between long phrases. The differences in skill between average and accomplished players is very pronounced on the oboe. The tone is so unique that it's best used as a solo voice, and it is most effective when the oboe enters alone and doesn't continue for very long. Like a strong spice, a little bit goes a long way. It is also very effective against subtle background colors. When using it as a sustained color in the background, stay in the middle register. The oboe blends well with itself, the English horn, the flute, the violin, and the viola. Typical oboe writing can be heard in Bizet's *Symphony in C*. The oboe has occasionally found its way into jazz. Recordings by the multiwoodwind jazz artist Yusef Lateeff make use of the oboe.

ENGLISH HORN

The English horn is a transposing instrument in F, and the parts are transposed up a perfect fifth. It shares the inherent strengths and problems of the oboe. The most characteristic moods of the English horn are dark, somber, or tragic. The English horn blends well with woodwind groups. Usually only one English horn is found in any ensemble. The English horn has a slightly slower response time than the oboe.

The bass oboe (heckelphone) can occasionally be heard. Delius's *A Dance Rhapsody* is a good example. There is also a sarrusophone, which is a metal-body contrabassoon. It is occasionally used with a group of oboes and English horns. The same considerations apply to these instruments.

CLARINETS

The B-flat clarinet is most common, and it transposes up a major second from concert pitch. There are other clarinets, in E-flat and A, but they are not as common.

Clarinets are very agile. Skips from one register to another are relatively easy. Staccato and legato phrases should coincide with natural breathing places. The range of the clarinet is very wide and can be divided into five distinct areas, each with its own characteristic sound (Example 7.7). Due to the acoustics of the instrument, notes in the area known as the "break" tend to sound somewhat stuffy. It is also somewhat difficult for all but the best players to play smoothly through this register from one side to the other. Another area to avoid—unless you are writing for virtuoso players—is the highest register, which contains many notes of questionable musical value.

Example 7.7: *Characteristics of the clarinet sound (at concert pitch, not transposed)*

The differences in register are more pronounced on B-flat clarinet than on any of the others. The high E-flat clarinet (piccolo clarinet) has a more shrill high register, where it can sound comical or humorous.

The bass clarinet is rich and deep in the lower register and doubles well with any low register orchestral instrument. Its overall response time is slower than the B-flat clarinet, but it can be very expressive on melodies and has a rich, full sound. The mid and upper registers are very expressive, but they are harder to control. The late jazz woodwind virtuoso, Eric Dolphy, made extensive use of the bass clarinet's expressive power.

The E-flat alto clarinet falls between the higher B-flat clarinet and the lower B-flat bass clarinet. It has qualities of both its neighbors but not with their extremes. The E-flat alto clarinet adds warmth and fullness to a group of clarinets. All the clarinets are natural for legato passages due to their facile qualities. Staccato should be clearly marked with additional suggestions or comments on the parts.

In sampling, a legato sample will not work on staccato passages, and fortissimo samples won't sound right at low-volume levels. There are many unusual things to use clarinet samples for if you have powerful editing capacities. A low note on the bass clarinet can be edited and used for a kick drum or low tom sound. Is it worth it, as an exercise in creative sound design? Who knows? Once you fully understand the rules, it's time to rewrite them methodically, if not break them outright.

BASSOON

The bassoon is a non-transposing instrument. The timbre of the bassoon is unmistakable. It is rich, woody, and very vocal. It has a wide range of expression, from mournful to comical. It has a particularly vocal quality in the upper part of its range.

The bassoon works well in thickening bass parts, where power is needed. As a melody instrument, it is naturally dramatic. Staccato works very well. Legato is relatively easy but not as easy as on clarinets or flutes.

The natural attack of the bassoon in the lower register is staccato, and that inhibits its ability to play softly. The upper register is very expressive and is good for lyrical melodies. The middle register has a

little less character. The low register is very intense and powerful. A cloth is occasionally stuffed into the bell to subdue the bassoon's power.

Fingerings on the bassoon are less slick than on other woodwinds, so check with your local virtuoso before writing a demanding part or unusual trills or effects.

The bassoon's timbre mixes well with other woodwinds and strings, especially in doubling viola or cello lines or in doubling violin lines an octave below. Some classic bassoon writing can be heard in *The Planets* by Holst (especially "Uranus") and *Symphony No. 8* by Dvořák as well as in Stravinsky's *Rite of Spring*. The contrabassoon and metal body sarrusophone sound an octave lower than written.

The Rite of Spring broke new ground in many ways. Bassoon players of the day thought he was crazy to write such unusual and high parts. They rose to the occasion and substantially reinvented the instrument. When the initial controversy over that piece of music subsided, we were left with new rules. History is full of examples of people who had the talent, technique, and patience to uncover new possibilities and to change the rules.

SAXOPHONE

The saxophone is the most flexible and vocal of the woodwinds. It is the only woodwind with a conical (versus cylindrical) bore. This fact allows for a wider range of personal expression and individual tone. With its flexibility, the saxophone a natural for jazz and pop music. The instrument is very responsive to the input and personality of its players. Because of this, it can easily be played poorly or sloppily. It can have a totally different sound depending on the player. The conical bore and a wide choice of mouthpiece styles give players a lot of room for adding their own personalities. Just compare the sounds of Paul Desmond, Dave Sanborn, John Coltrane, and Clarence Clemmon. Each saxophone also has a distinct personality. Representatives of many sounds and styles are found in the listening list at the end of this book.

The saxophone's flexibility makes its sounds very hard to synthesize. They are often useful only for occasional hits or for a few quick notes. Samples also share this problem. Constructing a long, legato synth or a sampled sax line that sounds realistic is almost impossible. When it is done, it is often devoid of the normal inflections, personality, and nuance that our ears take for granted with live players.

Recent developments in electronic wind instruments and synthesizers have created a new world for acoustic players to explore. MIDI based wind instruments that use synthesizers and samplers for sound sources are rapidly being perfected. They allow a tremendous amount of player input and control over all the parameters of sound and inflections. Many synths also offer breath controllers as options to give sounds more human input. Recent developments allow saxophone players to use their instruments as MIDI controllers, and they thereby have access to a new world of synthesized and sampled sounds.

CHAPTER EIGHT ✍
SMALL HORN SECTIONS

The decision to write horn parts for a piece of music is made in a general way before writing specific parts. After becoming familiar with the music, determine if the need for horn parts exists. Very often the style of music will make the decision obvious. Once you have decided to write horn parts, try asking yourself these questions:

1. Where are the strategic spots to place the horns located?

2. Describe the kind of parts you want to write. Are they sustained, high, low, melodic, syncopated, or short and punchy?

3. What instruments, players, or sounds would be appropriate? What's actually available?

4. How far can you stretch your imagination and still fulfill the needs of the assignment?

Getting down to specifics usually involves (1) the sounds, instruments, or players you will use; (2) the actual part (for example, lines or voicings); and (3) the orchestration (assigning sounds to notes).

Here's a typical arranging situation. You have made the decision to add some horn parts to a piece you are arranging or for someone else who has asked you to write horn parts. The process might proceed in the following way:

1. Learn the chord progression, harmonic rhythm, rhythmic structure, form, and style.

2. Learn the melody and background, or secondary melodies, and learn whether the piece is vocal or instrumental. More than any other element, the melody will indicate how, when, where, and why to write horn parts. Listening to the groove is important for determining the rhythmic character of the parts, but the parts must ultimately work with the melody.

3. Listen to how the singer (or instrumental soloist) interprets the melody. This can provide valuable ideas for horn parts. You may be able to incorporate some of these ideas into your parts.

4. Find all the open spaces or obvious places to fill with horns. Be sure that there is nothing else going on that could cause problems or conflicts in the arrangement. Find out what's expected.

5. If you are recording, how many tracks are available? This helps you plan your overdubs and doublings.

6. If the horn parts are intended for a live situation, what players or keyboards are available? Is the setup comfortable for players to hear and blend well? Can they see those they need to see for visual cues?

7. Be sure you don't write parts that exceed the abilities of the players or equipment. Find out as much as you can about the cast of characters, that is, if you are not doing everything yourself.

8. Don't be afraid to ask questions, especially if you are jumping in at the middle of someone else's project. Ask now or work twice as hard later. Assume nothing.

9. Before getting down to the details, make some sketches for the areas that need horns. This often involves writing out just the rhythms of the parts and not necessarily the notes. Try to hear the general shape and rhythmic content in your head. Don't worry about the details yet, just sketch through the piece in rough form. Your sketch is the outline you refer to as you fill in the details. The sketch firmly implants the big picture in your mind before you get lost in the details. It's easy to forget where you are going after spending hours on four bars of music. The sketch helps you keep perspective. (See Example 8.1 for a typical horn part.)

Last 4 of Verse
♩ = 120

voiced

2 trumpets, alto sax,
tenor sax, trombone

Example 8.1: *Sketch for writing horn parts*

Here's another typical arranging situation. You are ready to write horn parts for a pop tune, and you have got a sketch from which to work. Some of the parts are voiced, and some are unison or octave unisons. Let's assume the horn section is a mixed combination of saxes and brass, which is very common. Here's our imaginary combination: two trumpets, one tenor sax, one alto sax, and one tenor trombone. This gives us five horns. In a recording situation, these five horns can overdub additional harmonies or double existing parts. This is the most common way to get extra mileage out of the horn section.

Once you have actually written out the lines and voicings, it is time to decide who is going to play what notes. Not every voicing will have five notes, so it's likely that some instruments will play the same notes. Assuming that the voicings are balanced and well constructed to begin with, you now are faced with deciding how to assign the sounds to specific notes.

Example 8.2 will serve as the model voicing for this discussion. Here are some choices and suggestions: Voice the chord, from the top down, according to the natural ranges of the five horns. From the top down, the assignment of notes will look like Example 8.3, which will sound bright or brassy because the trumpets are on top. Notice the major second between D and E, which gives some extra bite or thickness to the voicing. The configuration in Example 8.4 will have a reedy sound because the saxes are on top and the trumpets are fairly subdued in their register. Example 8.5 alternates brass and reeds with alternating timbres on adjacent notes. Each instrument is in a full, comfortable part of its range. Example 8.6 makes the major second (D to E) more prominent because (1) the tenor sax is playing higher in relation to itself than the alto; and (2) the two saxes, which are instruments of the same family, are playing a relative dissonance. This highlights the major second more than if a brass and sax were playing the same two notes. The two saxes playing the major second (D to E) add some extra grit or bite to the voicing. Experiment with placing the tenor above the alto on the major second. Since both saxes are in full, comfortable spots in their range, they can be switched around.

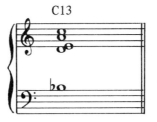

C13

Example 8.2: *Basic voicing for following examples*

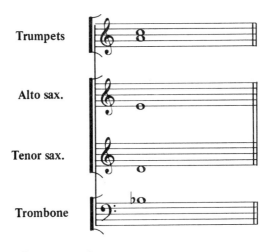

Trumpets

Alto sax.

Tenor sax.

Trombone

Example 8.3

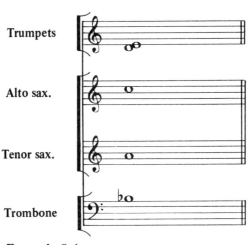

Trumpets

Alto sax.

Tenor sax.

Trombone

Example 8.4

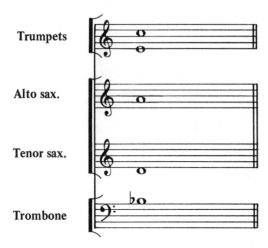

Example 8.5

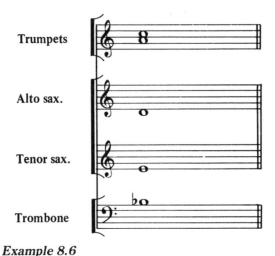

Example 8.6

Suggestions for Orchestration

NOTE ASSIGNMENTS

The most basic way to ensure trouble-free orchestration is to become familiar with the ranges and the keyboard versions of acoustic instruments. Assign sounds to notes that are characteristic and strong for their range and the part. Here is an illustration.

low instruments	low notes
mid-range instruments	mid-range notes
high-range instruments	high-range notes

This seems incredibly obvious, and it is. It also is virtually foolproof. The idea has continued to work well for centuries.

VARIED NOTE ASSIGNMENTS

There is much room for variation on the previous note assignments. The instruments' ranges have a lot of overlap. If you study the woodwind and brass range charts, you will see that with the exception of extreme ranges, many instruments' ranges coincide. This allows you to experiment with assigning a variety of available sounds to the same note and having many different and useful orchestrations. You will be surprised at how many colors you can get from a small horn section by shifting a few instruments or sounds to different notes.

The key to assigning notes is having a purpose. Have a sound in mind to guide your choice of orchestration. For example, if there are seconds in the voicing and you want to emphasize this, have a sound play one of the notes in a range where it is very colorful or unique, as opposed to its more neutral, mid-register areas. The best way to make this technique work is to have only one or two instruments out of their usual roles at a given time. Experiment, one sound at a a time, so you can hear the subtle differences in a controlled way. Players with good control and intonation or a wide selection of keyboard sounds will always make this easier. (See Example 8.7.)

Example 8.7: *Putting the baritone sax in its highest register, where it has a strong, reedy quality, highlights the minor second*

INTONATION

Acoustic instruments do not automatically play in tune by pushing buttons or moving fingers. Accuracy of pitch depends on several factors: (1) players must have well-developed concepts of pitch; (2) players must listen to each other and know what to listen for; and (3) players must be capable of and willing to make the subtle adjustments to compensate for the natural flaws in their instruments.

If you plan to use some colorful or unusual orchestration as in Example 8.7, consider surrounding the dissonant intervals with other instruments or sounds playing in more moderate registers. This gives a solid pitch reference to the player on a note that's most exposed. Players base part of their intonation on what's immediately around them. When adjacent notes are being played in comfortable registers, the exposed player has strong pitch references.

TOP NOTES

The choice of which instrument plays the top note of the voicing or unison depends on whether the chord or unison is an isolated or separate hit. The voice leading is then not an issue because it is not part of a moving line. Determine the timbre or color you want, and assign the instruments to the notes in a way that brings out the desired timbre. As an example, take a small horn section made up of two trumpets and one alto saxophone. Looking at the passage in Example 8.8, one option would be to put the alto sax on top of the two trumpets. This puts the saxophone at the very top of its range—which is all right for really strong players. This voicing produces a very bright, reedy quality.

Another option would put the sax under the two trumpets. Putting the trumpets in this higher register will lend more of a bright, brassy quality to the voicing.

The last option—one trumpet on top, alto sax in the middle, and the other trumpet on the bottom—has the two trumpets playing in sixths up to the last bar (where they are in fourths). This version has the least punch because the bottom trumpet is playing in its very neutral mid-range register.

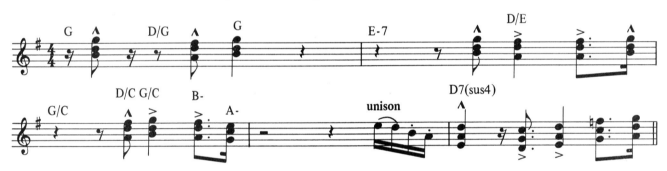

Example 8.8

Care must be taken even in voicing unison lines. If you wanted the ensemble of alto saxophone and two trumpets to play the unison line in Example 8.9, you would be in trouble because the last two notes are out of the range of the sax. The two solutions are shown in Example 8.10.

Also keep in mind the level of proficiency of your players: Although the unison line in Example 8.11 is playable on both trumpet and alto sax, the high A-flat in the first measure is the highest note available on the sax. Unless your part will be played by top-line players, it is probably better to write the first measure down and octave for the alto saxophone.

Example 8.10

Example 8.9

Example 8.11

CROSSING VOICES

In moving parts you must consider entire lines, and voice leading. You can assign one instrument to play the top notes (because all the notes fall in its range), or one sound may start the line and another sound may take its place later. This is called *crossing voices*.

It is particularly effective on a line that has a wide melodic range where no single instrument can cover the range. You can also use this as an interesting effect, even if one instrument can play all the top notes of the voicings or unison lines (Example 8.12 and 8.13).

Example 8.12

Line to be voiced

Voicing for two trumpets, alto sax, trombone

Example 8.13

COMBINATIONS OF UNISON AND VOICINGS

As mentioned earlier, one of the most effective writing techniques in any style is the unison, or octave unison. In writing for small horn sections, the unison is particularly dramatic. Saxes and brass combine extremely well at the unison because of their similar ranges, complementary timbres, and flexibility. Small horn sections are an integral part of all styles of commercial music. In fact, arrangers and producers specifically use live horns to provide contrast for heavily synthesized and sampled tracks. The human element is still as valuable as ever. One of the most common and powerful techniques is writing unison parts with occasional voicings. The occasional voicings highlight or emphasize particularly important or exposed areas. Some of the most common uses for these voicings are (1) emphasizing an important chord or harmonic rhythm; (2) emphasizing the ends of phrases; (3) emphasizing exposed punctuation (hits) or stabs; (4) adding extra thickness or grit to important harmonies; (5) emphasizing horn section solis or parts of an arrangement that feature the horn section, and (6) emphasizing transitions, interludes, intros, or modulations.

The use of unison or voicings is not determined by ironclad rules. Give two good arrangers the same horn section assignment, and there will be as many

differences as there are similarities. The most important thing is to write parts that add energy and create interest as they support the melody. Good arranging involves making decisions, planning a course of action, and executing ideas effectively. Experiment!

Another useful and dramatic effect is to voice a line that previously was unison. This is particularly effective in horn section solis, vamps, and fade endings. Bringing back an earlier unison line in a voiced version provides contrast, continuity, and power. In endings you will often hear the same line alternate between unison and voiced versions. For example, take a four-bar ending that repeats and fades for quite a while.

First four bars	Unison
Second four bars	Voiced
Third four bars	Unison, plus octave doubling
Fourth four bars	Voiced differently
Fifth four bars	Same voicing as second time, but with different orchestration. (The same sounds now play different notes in the voicing).

You can see the possibilities for variety and continuity. (See Example 8.14, which has various unison and voiced combinations.)

Example 8.14: *Unison and voiced versions of the same part—either of these parts (or a combination of the two) would work with any combination of brass and saxophones*

TEMPO

In general, the richer a voicing, the more time the ears need to absorb it. A rich or dense voicing has more information in it than a less dense voicing or a unison, so give people a chance to hear it.

The faster the tempo, the less dense your voicings should be, or else the dense voicings will need to sustain longer to be fully understood. This is another reason why unison is so effective and versatile. It works at any tempo. This reaffirms the importance of developing skills in writing melody, countermelody, and melodic motifs that can stand alone.

SPECIAL EFFECTS

Slurs, trills, glissando, grace notes, bends, and fall-offs are all possible in horn sections. Some are very easy, and others are hard, if not impossible. This is due to the physical construction of the instruments. There are as many exceptions as rules in this area, so the best way to learn is by asking the players, as well as by employing trial and error. Players can often approximate an effect if they can't execute it exactly. Be open to alternate suggestions from the people who play the instruments.

TRANSPOSITION

A mixed reed and brass horn section will have instruments with different transpositions. Become completely familiar with ranges and transpositions so that you are not writing parts that are awkward, unplayable, or written in the wrong octaves. Learn to visualize the notes as they will finally appear on the transposed parts. This is a must when you decide who will play what note. Even if you are playing these parts on keyboards, it is still important to do this. It helps make synth horns sound believable. When you spend hours writing parts, it's easy to forget about transposition. Think about the practicality of what you write. Memorize ranges and transpositions (See Example 8.15).

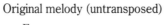

Original melody (untransposed)

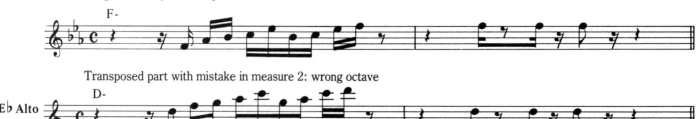

Example 8.15: *Common transposition errors*

Correctly transposed part includes difficult high G

Part is more effective an octave down

Example 8.15 *(continued)*

COPYING PARTS

Let's take a look at an all too familiar situation. You have just finished writing some great horn parts, and it is now time to transpose and copy parts. It's late and you are tired, so you decide to take some shortcuts in writing out individual parts. Right? Wrong! Shortcuts are just that; they cut your music short and create confusion. No one knows where to go next, the layout (roadmap) is confusing at best, there are transposition errors, and beats and measures are missing. "Yeah, but it all seemed to work fine when I wrote it!" There are standard, universally understood shortcuts illustrated at the end of this book. Refer to those for information on layout of parts. Here is a checklist for your parts.

1. Correct transposition

2. Accurate number of bars—each bar numbered (optional, but useful)

3. Rehearsal letters A, B, B^2, and so forth, placed clearly (preferably on the left-hand margin)

4. Phrasing, articulation, breath marks, special effects, dynamics clearly marked

5. Indicate any special or helpful instructions (for example, *vocals enter, watch conductor, listen to strings*).

6. Parts should indicate who else the player plays with or should listen to for any important reason. For example, on a sax part *unis. with trumpets* can be helpful when players are sight-reading or when you are assigning separate tracks or MIDI channels for each sound to your sequencer.

7. Indicate what section of the form is being played. Put this next to the rehearsal letters (A verse, B chorus, and so forth). In sections where the parts are *tacet* (silent) for more than a few measures, indicate the important lyrics or instrumental cues before players re-enter. If a player has been resting for thirty-two measures, it helps to know what someone else is playing or singing right before the entrance. Players appreciate seeing a line or two from the lyrics, or other parts cued in (written as a reminder to get ready). This is especially helpful when players are sight-reading.

8. If possible, subdivide long rest sections into smaller units. They are easier to count and keep track of this way. (See Example 8.16)

This long rest might be clearer if broken into two or more smaller ones

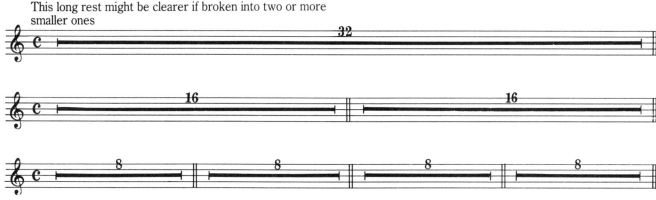

Example 8.16: *Subdividing long rests*

9. Horn sections usually have a leader, often the lead trumpet player. This person makes decisions about interpretation, phrasing, articulations and indicates cutoffs and entrances. They are like good coaches or quarterbacks who inspire great performances and bring the team together by earning the players' respect, not by demanding it.

10. If you are using keyboard horns, then you are the lead player (and all the others). This means your selection of sounds will have to accommodate all the nuances of the parts.

11. Horn parts for the same piece of music should be laid out the same way to expedite problem solving at rehearsals. Use the same number of bars or blocks of rests per line. Locate repeat marks at the same places. Locate first and second endings and D.S. and D.C. markings in the same places. If measures are numbered, use the same method for all parts.

ENDINGS, VAMPS, OPEN SECTIONS, INTERLUDES, AND TRANSITIONS

These sections are often where the more adventurous or involved horn parts occur. Usually this is because the melody is resting or ad-libbing in a way that leaves the horn parts more room to develop without conflict.

In these sections you can voice lines that were previously unison, or you can rhythmically, melodically and harmonically explore the implications of earlier parts. Again, choose one or two ideas and develop them fully. Here's an idea for open sections or vamps. Let's say you have a four-bar horn part that will repeat indefinitely. Write another part three bars long that contrasts with but is compatible with the first part. The four-bar phrase will repeat three times in twelve bars. The three bar phrase will repeat four times in twelve bars. So every twelve bars you will complete the cycle, building an interesting tension. You can accomplish this in several ways.

1. Divide the horn section into two smaller horn sections.

2. Let the synth horns be one section, and let the acoustic (or other synth horns) be the other section.

3. In a recording situation you can overdub the additional horn section using any sound combination you want.

What we are aiming for here are two similar sections that will play related parts of different phrase lengths. Example 8.17 illustrates this idea.

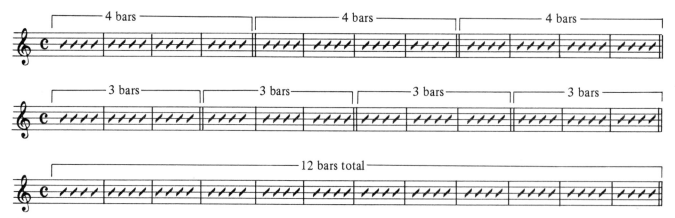

Example 8.17: *Unequal phrase lengths*

Look for any number that has odd and even multiples. (For example, 20 bars = 4 × 5 or 5 × 4; and 24 bars = 6 × 4, 4 × 6 or 3 × 8, 8 × 3.) This technique works best when the sections have similar lengths. (For example, 4 bars with 5 bars [20] and 3 bars with 4 bars [12]). Sections of similar length make the technique sound deliberate, rather than random or accidental. This will work well in any group of compatible sounds. If you keep the parts well defined and fairly simple, it can add fresh life to an arrangement.

Orchestrating Pedal Point or Ostinato

A nonstop (sequencer) line can be written for horn sections. It is simple to get the line played without the players being out of breath. First of all, determine that this is the effect you want. If it is, divide the part between two or more players of the same instrument. Have one instrument play the first part of the phrase and another player of the same instrument play the next part of the phrase. This is similar to passing a hot potato between two people. This is also effective with different sounds or instruments (Example 8.18).

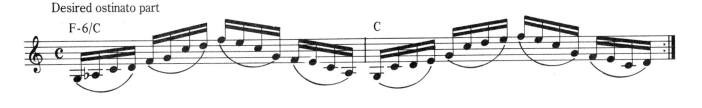

Example 8.18: *Ostinato divided between two instruments*

Acoustic horn players can sustain notes only as long as they are able to hold their breaths. But if players stagger (alternate) entrances on sustained notes, then one person is always playing while another person pauses for a breath. A group of players on the same or different instruments can sustain pedal notes indefinitely by alternating entrances and breaths. Adding dynamics to this note, creates the effect of expanding and contracting. (See Example 8.19.)

Example 8.19: *Pedal point with overlapping entrances and staggered breathing*

RELATIVE DYNAMICS

Dynamic markings are assumed to be relative to the instrument and the register in which it plays. For example, two trumpets playing a fortissimo high C will be louder than two saxes playing fortissimo on the same note an octave lower. Balancing dynamics in a group means interpreting dynamic markings in relation to context. Players need to learn the music and treat dynamics as guidelines adjusted according to the needs of the music and the players.

It's not unusual to give the various instruments their own dynamics for the same section of music to compensate for their differences. Trumpets playing a high C might have a mezzo forte, while saxes on the same note may have a forte or fortissimo to achieve the same intensity. (See Example 8.20.) Players achieve dynamic balance by adjusting their volumes so that their notes blend into the group. Knowing the players' strengths and weaknesses allows you to fine tune and personalize parts. Some trumpet players can play in the high register with such full, rich sounds and control that the notes sound lower than they really are. The notes are high, but they don't sound strained. Other players make the same notes sound twice as high or difficult to play.

The sax parts are marked fortissimo to compensate for the trumpets being in a naturally loud register

Example 8.20: *Relative dynamics*

A centered sound is easier for others to play in tune with and also projects further and doesn't distort. There is a solid, stable core to the sound, making the pitch of the note easy to hear. A focused sound will project further than a spread sound and will stay focused longer than a spread sound does at any distance.

A major factor of blend is having focused, tuned sounds with which to work. Spread sounds dissipate quickly and never have a chance to blend at any volume. The most desirable part of any sound is its quality (*timbre*). Once the sound is focused, then volume becomes an easy issue to deal with.

Many horn players are expanding their repertoire of sounds by using the new MIDI based woodwind and brass synth interfaces. There are new pitch-to-MIDI converters, and breath controllers for synths. There are even MIDI adapters for saxophones that allow them to control a MIDI keyboard. In this way, horn players can control MIDI keyboards from the instruments with which they feel most comfortable. The worlds of electronic and acoustic horns are getting closer by the minute.

Additional Suggestions

One of the best ways to learn about horn section arranging is by doing a lot of transcription. Part of your study should involve transcription. It is wonderful ear-training, and it will provide much insight as to what works and why.

There are many great horn section arrangers. Trumpet player–arranger Jerry Hey is one of the most prolific and talented. You can hear his work on albums by Al Jarreau; Earth, Wind, and Fire; Manhattan Transfer; Dream Girls; and many more. Also look into classic Motown and Stax Records, Tower of Power, the Brecker Brothers, Huey Lewis, and The System's album *Don't Disturb This Groove,* which features the New West Horns. You can also find continual inspiration by listening to masters such as Duke Ellington, Ray Charles, Gil Evans, Count Basie, and Hot Five. (See the listening list at the end of this book.)

If you can, organize a rehearsal band on your own or in conjunction with several other arrangers. Try to get players who are anxious to play so that you will feel free to experiment. Part of learning to write is willingness to take chances. If you always play it safe because you are worried about what the players think, you will cut your growth short. If a live situation is out of the question, rest assured that your sequencer and keyboards will never judge you or make wisecracks. We never outgrow the need for intelligent, constructive criticism from our peers.

Another good exercise is to write horn parts for records that don't have any. Make believe you have been asked to arrange horn parts for the song. Make a tape of the existing song and overdub your parts onto empty tracks of your work tape.

After you have done all you can to make your synth horns sound terrific, switch your keyboards to various nonpitched percussive sounds. Using the sequencer, play the horn parts back with these or any other nonpitched sounds. Now you hear the rhythmic content of the parts.

Try experimenting with the vari-speed function on a multitrack recorder to change the character of your parts. If you are going to use horns in a noncharacteristic way, try this new approach. If you want the horns to sound really unusual, make the parts different enough so they don't sound like mistakes or half-hearted attempts. Allow yourself to experiment in a big way. If it works, you will know it; and if it flops, you will know that too! At least you will be one step closer to the final solution. Finally here are some suggestions from top New York studio and jazz saxophonist Ken Hitchcock.

These are some of the most important things any arranger can do when they write for a horn section: Make sure the parts are singable. This has to do with letting them breathe and phrase naturally. Be conscious of the ranges and registers of each instrument. Remember to consider how important transposition is. A part may look okay on a concert score, but the only thing that counts is the final, transposed part. Avoid any large skips or jumps. Smooth, logical voice leading works best. It's the safest way to make parts playable. What works on a keyboard may not be technically possible for some horns. Keep the horns in appropriate registers for the parts. If a horn section is forced to play their instruments louder than they are meant to be, then the blend, sound quality, and pitch are lost. The volume has to be comfortable to blend and to lock in on the time.

Horn sections get a good blend when the voicings are well written. Big spaces between notes ruin the blend. Playing perfectly in tune means being adaptable to other horn players as well as to the rest of the band, or track. Good players play their instruments well in tune, but there are always going to be fine adjustments, so stay flexible.

I think most keyboard-oriented arrangers should invite comments and suggestions from horn players in order to make their parts more realistic. Depending on the key of an arrangement, it may be effective to modulate for horn solos or horn section solis. This can create excitement or put the horn(s) in a stronger key for that particular section. For example, certain keys make it easier to play the screaming high notes on saxophone solos. Some arrangements can really benefit from changing key, while others are already in keys that place the instrument in exciting registers.

CHAPTER NINE ✍
WRITING FOR THE RHYTHM SECTION

Groove or feel in a rhythm section is the result of the interaction between the basic elements. These elements are the drums, basic rhythm guitar and keyboard parts, bass line, and any other part that is essential to the foundation. "Basic" means parts that occur consistently throughout entire sections if not whole arrangements. Drum fills, solos, melodic fills, and incidental percussion are not basic elements of a groove, important as they are to an arrangement. The basic rhythm section parts (whether played, sequenced, or both) form the foundation upon which the rest of the arrangement is built.

Building Rhythm Section Grooves

There is no set way of building a groove. We often assume that the writing of every arrangement begins by developing a solid drum part first. A more realistic way of looking at this is that most pop arrangements have a solid drum groove at their base, but that doesn't mean that the drum parts were developed or conceived first.

Songwriters, arrangers, and producers often begin with a riff or idea on some other instrument and later experiment with drum ideas. In current pop recording it is very common to have drummers or programmers make their contributions after the other elements of a track are in place. This allows the drums to react to established parts and add some feeling while tying all the elements together. Sync-to-tape features or replacing guide-drum tracks make this process relatively easy and allow you to experiment with drum grooves, as you do with any other part.

There are many ways to build rhythm section grooves. Players can jam together around a simple riff or you can methodically program and sequence. There

is no single correct way. The best way is the way that works best for you on a given project. For those people who work with sequencers, drum machines, and keyboards (as opposed to live rhythm sections), there are ways to get a more human or relaxed feeling into the basic groove parts. Many sequencers allow you to offset any part rhythmically. For example, you can move a bass line slightly ahead or behind the center of the beat. This allows parts to breathe or have a more human quality. Most great human rhythm sections are "rock steady," yet they still flex or breathe with the music. It is common for different sections of an arrangement to have slight variations in tempo. For example, a chorus may be as much as a few beats per minute (bpm) faster than the preceding section. These subtle changes are not always planned by live players. They usually occur because the music feels like it needs to flex, accelerate, or relax a bit. Players make these subtle adjustments unconsciously as they collectively interact with the music.

You can simulate this by programming minor tempo changes into your MIDI gear. The slight variations in tempo can make machine-based tracks feel somewhat more human. Experiment with minor tempo changes combined with offsets.

People tend to work out rhythm section parts on whatever instruments they feel most comfortable with. As you become familiar with more equipment, you will be able to work out rhythm section ideas using different instruments. This will also give you more of a gut feeling for what rhythm section players do.

Transcription is one of the most powerful techniques for learning about rhythm sections and grooves. Pick some records where the playing is relatively straightforward and well recorded. It's important to hear all the parts. Transcribe and analyze as much as you can, and do it on a regular basis. You will be amazed at how much you learn about each instrument's role after dissecting a few rhythm tracks.

If you can, put together a rehearsal band and work on original and cover material. Concentrate on developing clear, well-defined parts that interact with the others.

When you think about building rhythm section parts, the subject of time (in the pure sense) comes up. In music of constant tempo, each beat has a length of its own, with a definite beginning, middle, and end. There also is space between each beat. Interpretation has a lot to do with where in the time you play (or sequence). In a constant tempo, think of individual beats as circles, spaced equidistant from the next circle, as shown below.

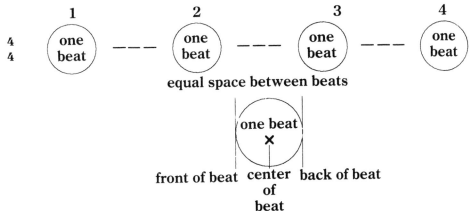

Playing and interpreting music with an emphasis on different places within the beat has a major influence on the feel or groove of the music, as shown here.

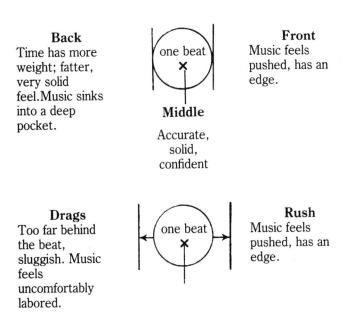

Back
Time has more weight; fatter, very solid feel.Music sinks into a deep pocket.

Middle
Accurate, solid, confident

Front
Music feels pushed, has an edge.

Drags
Too far behind the beat, sluggish. Music feels uncomfortably labored.

Rush
Music feels pushed, has an edge.

From these two diagrams you can see that metronomic time still has flexibility within each beat and measure. Tempo is a big factor, too. The faster the tempo, the smaller the spaces between the beats and the less flex each beat has. It's been said that one of the hardest things to do with time in pop music is to play a slow-groove ballad and make it feel good. There is so much distance between the beats when a tempo is slow that it takes that much more control to hold back without dragging. This is part of the art of groove playing. In your analytical listening and transcription make an effort to become conscious of how the various parts are being interpreted within the time. For example, in a rhythm section that feels "laid back" or relaxed, not necessarily all the parts are being played (sequenced) in back of the beat. Often only one or two elements are sufficient to impart that feeling. If a rhythm section feels on top of the beat, try to hear which elements are creating that feeling. Feel and groove are as much a result of interpretation as they are a result of the parts themselves.

In fact "laying back" or playing "on top" are most effective when some parts do and others don't. This way there is a desirable tension or contrast within the rhythm section. The slight contrast or discrepancy in the interpretation of the time from one part to the next calls attention to the feeling or groove and gives the part character.

One last thought on this subject. There is no single type of interpretation that is inherently superior to others. The feel of a particular arrangement may change slightly from day to day. A strong piece of music will withstand any number of interpretations. The feel in sequenced music will be determined by the flexibility of the technology and by how clever and conscious you are in manipulating it. If you are sequencing your rhythm section parts, experiment with offsets on one part at a time, relating the change back to the whole.

The development of a rhythm section groove happens as parts are added to whatever already exists. Parts are developed in reaction or relation to previous parts. A part you are working on will often conflict with a previous part, and you will end up revising the old part to accommodate the new one. When your rhythm parts are in the development stage, it helps not to get too attached to any part before the experimenting is done. Don't be afraid to revise early ideas to accommodate new ones. Do whatever it takes to get the strongest rhythm section groove. This may mean writing or playing the most simple parts and leaving room for other parts to fit in. The old cliché "less is more" is very appropriate. No matter how busy or slick something sounds, if it really works, it probably contains well-crafted, simple parts that also have strong enough musical identities to stand alone.

When a live rhythm section gets together to

work on the groove for an arrangement, lots of ideas fly around until a common denominator is found. Ideally, the needs of the music should transcend the dominating needs of any individual ego. If all your ideas don't get into one arrangement, they will find their place soon enough.

A rhythm section of players who are musically and personally compatible makes it easier and quicker to refine individual parts into a coherent whole. This is one reason why a strong rhythm section of players who are used to each other is an arranger's or a producer's dream. People who groove together musically and personally can quickly take music to new heights in a cost-effective way.

If you work alone, you are interacting with yourself and the equipment. As you write and sequence the parts, be conscious of interpreting the parts in addition to executing them. Think like a player as well as a programmer, no matter what sound you are using. Put some body language into it so you can feel the part. Play some "air" drums, bass, or guitar.

Range   **Open strings**

Both guitar and bass sound an octave lower than written.

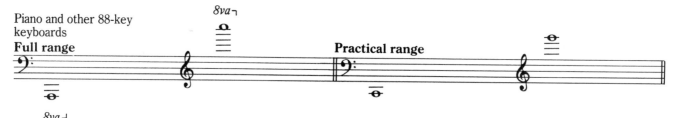

Example 9.1: *Ranges of rhythm section instruments*

Bass

In pop music bass parts are played on either keyboards or electric bass. Traditional jazz uses string bass, although recent jazz and jazz-fusion groups make use of any and all bass instruments. Electric basses have frets or are fretless. Each one has its own unique sound. Signal processing has an important role in shaping many bass sounds, and there are certain types of bass parts that depend on effects or processing to sound complete. In these cases the sound, part, and effects are totally integrated.

Certain bass lines sound best sequenced and played with specific keyboard sounds that are very different from electric bass sounds. In this case the idea is to develop a part and sound that does not imitate an electric bass. On the other hand there are certain styles and parts that only sound right when a human being plays the bass.

Finally, there are parts where sequencing or live playing are equally appropriate from a musical and technical point of view. The parts lend themselves to a variety of sounds and approaches. At this point, the decision is made by personal preference, availability of players, or economics.

There are styles of music that have evolved around drum machines and sequenced bass parts. This is an interesting chicken-or-egg situation. Do the sequenced bass lines develop because new sounds seem to lend themselves to these parts, or are writers and players constantly coming up with parts that require the development of new sounds to fit them? The answer is that both situations are true.

All bass parts have characteristics in common, no matter what instrument is used. First, bass parts are found in the lower registers. This is where the roots of the chords are in the harmonic series, and it makes sense to have the roots play where they have the greatest power to anchor the harmony. Bass parts played in higher registers don't sound like bass parts. Again, the sound and register are critical if the part is to be effective. A bass part played in a high register will clash with parts intended for that register. Just imagine a kick-drum part played up two octaves. It might be interesting, but it won't sound like a kick drum any more. Bass parts outline the roots of chords or function as pedal tones or ostinati.

A second characteristic is that the bass parts and the kick drum are usually the lowest pitches in a pop arrangement. They occupy the same registers and have much in common from an acoustic standpoint. It comes as no surprise that they also are rhythmically very connected and often play the same rhythms. It's also common for rhythmically active bass lines to play independently of the kick drum in some places and then to coincide on important downbeats, accents, or syncopations. Take the time to transcribe bass parts and kick-drum parts and compare them. Find the similarities and variations. Modern recording techniques make these parts very clear and easy to hear. Start with records that have simple grooves and parts. Listen to each part separately and then try to hear the bass line and kick drum together. Listen to how they play in unison or bounce off of each other. Remember that acoustic and electric bass sounds an octave lower than written. Synth bass will sound as written or not depending on the way the patches are set up or the keyboard is transposed. (See Example 9.2.)

Circles indicate rhythmic unisons.

Example 9.2: Kick-drum/bass part

There are several types of bass parts that are the basis for almost everything we hear in pop music. Almost any bass part can be described in one one of the following ways:

1. The part is rhythmically active or inactive. Active does not mean the parts have to be syncopated, although they can be.

2. The part is harmonic (active or inactive). This means that the part is root-oriented. It moves actively or inactively from root to root with few or no passing tones or embellishments (Example 9.3).

Inactive-harmonic bass part

Active-harmonic bass part

Example 9.3

3. The part is melodic (active). In addition to outlining the roots, these parts have passing tones or embellishments that give them a strong melodic contour. They look and sound like melodic lines outlining the chords and contain a greater variety of notes and rhythmic activity than harmonic parts. Melodic bass lines, by their very nature, are at least somewhat active and more complex (Example 9.4).

Active-melodic bass part

Example 9.4

Keyboard Parts

Although this section is focused on developing keyboard parts, much of the information applies to guitar parts, too.

Keyboard parts are active or sustained. Pad parts don't supply any rhythmic energy in an arrangement, but they do provide backdrops for all the other active parts. The decisions about whether to use pad parts or not, or in what sections, has to do with the style of music and personal taste. There are many records that have few or no pad parts but still sound full. The other parts imply the harmony, or several parts collectively outline the harmony in such a way that pads are not ever missed. A thick-voiced pad part can take up a lot of space in an arrangement or mix. There are also many transparent sounds that you almost feel rather than hear. These are very useful in that they provide a subtle backdrop without swallowing up all the other parts. Pads are usually in the middle register where the voicings are most full.

Basic keyboard parts are frequently rhythmic. They are the comps or riffs that are recognizable "hooks" in an arrangement. These are the essential active parts that provide rhythmic energy. When you work out the rhythms for keyboard comp parts, it is important to be conscious of certain factors. First, find suitable sounds for the part. Have a general idea of the type of sounds you want and how full or big the part should be. In active-syncopated comp parts, match the sound to the part and to the density of the voicings. Second, avoid playing active left-hand parts in conjunction with pads or rhythmic comps. They usually crowd or conflict with bass parts or create a muddy, undefined lower registers. Leave your left hand out, or use it to play in the middle register with the right-hand part.

An overactive left hand is a common problem for keyboard players, especially for those who are used to playing piano accompaniments, solo piano jobs, or in situations where they are required to be one-person orchestras. If necessary, force yourself to play with one hand at a time. Nonetheless, there are several situations where the keyboard part depends on left-and right-hand interaction.

For example, it occurs in pianistic parts. This style of playing is found in pop ballads, rubato intros, or any section of an arrangement where most of the activity is limited to the melody and keyboard accompaniment. This is where you hear "real" piano parts that use the full range, inflection, and character of the piano. Often the bass part is silent, sustains, or is an integral part of the piano part. Left-hand and right-hand interaction is also important in two-handed rhythmic syncopated comps. In these cases the left hand usually plays in a rhythm that complements the bass part. The part is usually written an octave higher than the bass; however, if the left-hand part is in the same octave as the bass, the sound really needs to be different to avoid muddiness. "Funky" clavinet parts are common examples of this.

Using two-handed keyboard comps requires you to be very conscious of potential conflicts in sound and register with the bass part. For example, if the bass sound is very deep and thick, try a brighter, less dense sound on the keyboard part.

Keyboard sounds and parts usually change from one section to another. This way each section has its own color and identity. Secondary keyboard parts should have their own unique musical shapes and sounds to avoid cluttering the basic keyboard parts.

It's also very common to reinforce a part with lots of MIDI layers. This has to be done carefully. Having sixteen keyboards play the same part is not going to make the part sixteen times better. In fact, due to the acoustics of the situation (for example, phase cancellation) your sound may end up smaller and less defined than with a few carefully planned MIDI layers.

Another way to reinforce a part is simply by highlighting the accents, syncopations, or important downbeats. For example, you might have a high-register bell sound outlining the top notes of your voicings or accenting certain important chords. This creates the illusion of fullness without unwanted thickness.

In any pop record there often are several elements occurring simultaneously in the same general register. The reason this works (when it does) is that each part has its own distinct sound and melodic and rhythmic identity. If it's not working, you can be sure one or more parts lacks identity or is somehow conflicting with the others. Here's a typical example. All the parts—lead vocal, soft-string pad, clean-guitar part, rhythmic keyboard comp, pitched percussion (marimba sound playing broken sixteenth-note pattern) —occur in the middle register. Thus there are five different things going on simultaneously. How do we make it work? Each part has a different sound and rhythmic and melodic character. Each part also has its own place in the stereo image (mix) with its own ambience and signal processing to further define and place it. This is by no means an open invitation to load up the middle register with the assumption that you can fix it in the mix. The parts must first work musically; then you can place, separate, and enhance them in the mix.

Arrangers who are primarily keyboard players often overdo it with keyboard pads and comps and secondary parts because they know their instruments' capabilities well, hear so many possibilities at once, have good technique, and have many great sounds. It's a challenge to get everything cranking away! The real challenge, however, is to play what's needed and weed out the rest. Sometimes people with minimal technique come up with great and often useful comps and parts because that's all their technique allows. Their parts are economical but so very right. The most important lesson we can learn is restraint. It's much easier to add parts to an arrangement that is too sparse than to thin out and revise one that is overwritten. MIDI makes it easier than ever to overwrite and over comp. Try the following routine when you develop primary keyboard pad or comp parts: Write and play the most stripped-down version of what you hear. (You can always add on later.) If

the part still comes out active, ask yourself if the part might not be more effective divided among several other sounds. It is so common to hear an interesting part in our heads, especially one that is rhythmically active and well defined. We may not recognize that it's really two or more related parts. See if the part is effective when divided among several timbres.

There are many ways to develop interesting pad and comp parts. When you first play through a chord progression, the normal routine goes something like this. Choose a neutral sound (for example, a pianolike sound) and play a simple pad part through the chords, catching whatever syncopations are already indicated in the harmonic rhythm. In this way you walk through the progression, get the lay of the land, and gather ideas. After doing this a few times, you will begin to develop a part with some rhythmic character and contrast that will bring some energy to the progression. Or, you might decide that a very simple inactive pad part is really best. You will also remember that other parts will be developed on top of your pad or comp, so you are always trying for the lowest common denominator.

One way to add rhythmic life to an otherwise static pad is to arpeggiate the chords. In conjunction with this, try adding some tensions to the chords (Example 9.5). Another way to add rhythmic energy is to play the chords in repeating quarter, eighth, or sixteenth notes with a pattern of syncopated accents. This sets up a subtle "time within the time," similar to adding syncopated accents to a hi-hat/shaker part (Example 9.6).

Example 9.5

Example 9.6: *Accent pattern for arpeggiated part*

For those of you who have access to recording equipment, try using the key-input of a noise gate. By doing this, you can key a sustained pad part to your active hi-hat, and the pad will then "percolate" in the same rhythm and accents of the hi-hat. This is a useful production technique that allows you to create rhythmic activity where it never was in the original performance.

Major chords in current pop music are often voiced by omitting the third and adding the second (ninth); or else the added second can shift to and from the third. Minor chords often alternate the ninth and eleventh with the third and fifth. For example, C− may also use a B♭/C to C− pattern. The D and F of the B♭ chord are the ninth and eleventh of the C− chord. (For further versions, see Example 9.7.) If you do choose to go with a sustained pad, the choice of sounds becomes all-important. The sound is everything because there is no other activity to sustain the listener's interest.

Example 9.7

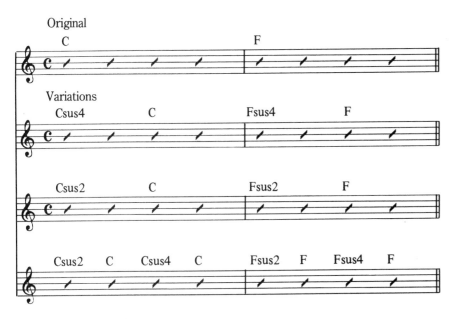

Example 9.7 (continued)

In addition to the pad and comp versions, there are often secondary parts that fit over these parts. A common part is an eighth- or sixteenth-note arpeggiated and pitched percussion part. Find a percussion sound (for example, marimba) and write and sequence an active part, either in unison or voiced. Intervals of fourths sound particularly good on this type of part (Example 9.8).

Example 9.8: Arpeggiation using constant fourths

Last, but not least, are the single-line melodic fills that answer the melody, or the "bell" sounds that highlight the top notes in voicings. One way to keep some daylight, or open space, in both your keyboard parts and in the arrangement in general is to have the basic keyboard comp play the rhythmic accents of the harmony without sustaining through to the next chord change. This is a way of playing or outlining the harmonic rhythm and still leaving some space. It often involves playing the downbeats, accents, or syncopations while remaining silent in between. This almost minimalist approach works well on arrangements that are busy and that have several parts in the same register. It leaves room for the unusual sounds, parts, and textures that add interest. The silence, or space, has beauty and merit of its own and is just as important and powerful as the music around it. Space is not something to be filled automatically or compulsively. If your keyboard parts end up being very sparse, maybe that's all you need and anything else would be clutter. There is the unfortunate misconception (especially among people who hire arrangers) that the music is not good unless the score and parts are crammed full of millions of notes. The people who pay for such arrangements and production feel this is the only way to get their money's worth. This theory is deeply flawed. An arrangement should only be busy when the music warrants it. Don't feel that your work is inadequate unless you have a million notes flying around. In fact, having breathing space in your arrangements is an admirable goal (Example 9.9). Consider the space to be an equal priority.

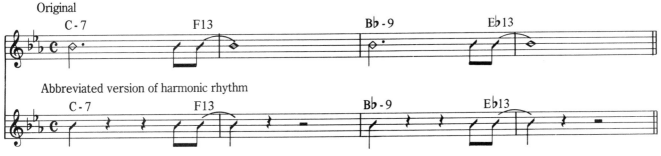

Example 9.9

Some contemporary masters that use space as an important musical part are producer-arrangers, Arif Mardin, Kashif, Narada Michael Walden, Maurice White, David Foster, Gino Vanelli, Jimmy Jam and Terry Lewis, Don Sebesky, Gil Evans, Duke Ellington, and Thad Jones, to name a few. Here are some interesting and useful observations by two top keyboard-players/arrangers/producers.

I have found that a flexible approach toward keyboard arrangements is most successful. When an arranger allows the synthesist to change a voicing, subtract or add notes, change octaves, or try other patches, great things can happen. I was once sequencing a dance record where one of the synth parts was a sixteenth-note machinelike part. I spent a good hour trying to make the idea work. I was still not happy. After returning from a break, I turned all the synths back on, and one did not return to its previous patch. I started the sequencer and the part was now two octaves lower and sounded great! I then proceeded to "clean up" the spots where it clashed with the bass. That was a lucky accident that is a valuable lesson. If time and budget allow, go with the ideas rather than hold on to every note. *Alec Shantzis*

Developing rhythm section parts is like putting together a jigsaw puzzle. I try to get the general shape or picture by first really learning the song. Then I work on the kick-drum and bass parts together, filling in the backbeats (two and four) as needed and work my way up to the hi-hat–shaker parts. Very often a new part will negate something I worked on earlier, so I try not to get too attached to any part when I'm at this stage. I'm willing to allow new ideas to require modifying or letting go of previous parts.

One big difference between arranging now as compared to a few years ago is that signal processing has really become important in shaping sounds and parts in the writing stage. The outboard equipment is so flexible that once you understand it, it really plays a central role in developing musical parts. I tend to think of the part, sound, and processing as one at the writing stage, whereas it used to be common to think of processing only at the mix. I may not record the part with effects, but I usually have certain effects in mind when I'm writing. I'll even include info about the processing when I write parts or scores. *Alan Zahn*

Guitar

Everything mentioned in the keyboard section also applies specifically or generally to guitar parts and sounds. Guitars are either acoustic (with hollow bodies) or have solid bodies. There are also semiacoustic (hollow) guitars that have smaller acoustic resonating spaces than the totally acoustic guitars. Acoustic guitars can be amplified by playing into a mic or having a pickup(s) mounted over the hole or internally. Solid body guitars transmit their sounds through any number of magnetic pickups mounted on their bodies. Guitars are played into mics, amps, amps that are mic'd, directly into mixers, or any combination of these. A wide variety of signal processing and effects are available in various combinations to shape sounds.

The guitar is a particularly difficult instrument for which to write detailed linear parts. Due to the way the fingerboard is laid out, there are many ways to play the same note. If you are not at least familiar with its basic layout, writing for the guitar can be like playing three-dimensional tic-tac-toe. It's very easy to write a line or part that works well on keyboard, but the same part may present fingering problems on the guitar.

It helps to think of guitar parts and sounds as belonging to two general categories—clean or distorted. There are many types of clean guitar sounds and effects, as there are a wide variety of distorted sounds and effects. Clean parts have a clear, undistorted sound, even when processed with chorus, delay, flanging, or compression. Distorted guitar sounds are overdriven, crunchy, thick, or dirty sounds that we have come to associate with rock guitar. Distortion of guitar sounds can be accomplished by overdriving an amp (turning the volume way up) or by using one of the many effects boxes that simulate the sound of an amp being moderately overdriven or set all the way on stun.

Any type of guitar sound is dependent on some or all of the following:

1. Use of and thickness of a pick
2. Use of fingers
3. Place of attack in the playing area
4. Tone controls
5. Combination of pickups (with tone controls)
6. Phase of pickups
7. Types of pickups
8. Type of construction—materials, dimensions
9. Amp characteristics (size and number of speakers, tubes or transistors)
10. Signal processing—effects. (There are effects processors that are primarily for distortion as well as many others that are effectively used in both categories and in any number of combinations
11. Mic placement, direct input (both together)
12. The player—always the most important

DISTORTED SOUNDS AND PARTS

Most seasoned guitarists will find the next few sections to be quite obvious. For arrangers and writers who play other instruments, these paragraphs are designed to fill in some blanks.

There are many levels of distortion. The stereotypical overdriven guitar parts are power chords and screaming lead lines or solos. Power chords are essentially written in a low- to midregister and they are perfect fifths (a very resonant interval) or single notes played with a mild to heavily distorted sound. Power chords are usually sustained or not very active rhythmically. The sounds themselves, played in perfect fifths, are too dense and have too much sustain for agile parts (Example 9.10).

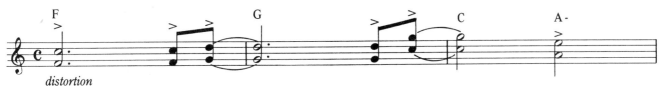

If fifths are too dense, use single notes

Example 9.10 *Guitar power chords (as written)*

However, a distorted sound works incredibly well for expressive, rock-oriented solos. The sustain of the sound allows for a wide range of emotional and technical expression, especially in mid-to-high registers where the guitar has especially vocal qualities.

Not all distorted guitar sounds need the extreme settings on amps or the effects that (among other sounds) simulate an amp being overdriven. It's very common to take a clean sound and bring it gradually toward distortion. This is done by using less radical amp or effects settings. Moderately distorted sounds are useful in power chords, solos, lead lines, and rhythm guitar parts involving chord strumming, arpeggiation, or single note rhythmic parts. Moderate distortion allows for increased flexibility because the sound is less dense than maximum overdrive. The level of distortion is determined by the need of the part and by the surrounding context.

The greater the amount of distortion, the larger a space that part will consume in a mix or performance. Maximum distortion is capable of acting like a sponge in the mix. It will soak up almost any sound in its register. If your music calls for serious distortion, be sure the other parts have maximum contrast and are in other registers. Delicate sounds and subtle nuances get lost under such a sound.

These are some guidelines for working with distorted sounds.

1. Start at minimum distortion and work your way up before cranking up the afterburner or setting your controls on stun.

2. You may find that the amount of distortion you have is fine. What you really need to do is make E.Q. or guitar pickup adjustments to give you the presence or tonal coloration you want. Don't go for the max until you've tried some of these other adjustments.

3. Check to see that you haven't obliterated the rest of the music. Some styles and parts call for maximum overdrive, which is fine. Make sure you are aware of who or what is playing in the same register. Establish priorities. If you don't, maximum overdrive will negate much of what is in the same register.

Here are examples of some typical distortion parts.

1. Solos

2. Power chords

3. Single sustained lines

4. Single-note active comps—muted or open quarter, eighth, or sixteenth notes with syncopated accents

5. Chord comps that are not power chords (fifths)

6. Melodic fills or licks used as background parts

7. Arpeggiated parts

Artists and groups with typical distorted guitar sounds and parts include the following:

1. Eddie Van Halen
2. Boston (Tom Scholz)
3. Jimi Hendrix
4. Eric Clapton
5. Toto
6. Rolling Stones
7. Mister Mr.
8. Bryan Adams
9. Heart
10. Journey
11. Foreigner
10. Les Paul
11. Chet Atkins
12. Buddy Holly
13. Madonna

CLEAN GUITAR SOUNDS

We can probably say that the cleanest guitar sound comes from an acoustic guitar. There are no electronics to color the sound. Moving away from the pure acoustic guitar sounds we find a variety of semiacoustic or solid-body guitars capable of a wide range of sounds, from clean to overdriven.

With electric guitars, the primary clean sound is the instrument played through an amp or a direct line into a mixing console. The sound is a combination of the instrument (pickups, tone controls) and the tonal coloration that the amp or console gives.

Clean sounds can be further colored by any or all of the following nondistortion devices: chorus, flange, delay, compression-limiting, phase shift, pitch shift, and doubling. Any of these, in any combination, will alter the sound, yet it will still be clean and clear compared to the distortion sounds.

Clean guitar sounds do not consume the space in a mix that distorted sounds do. This does not mean that an overwritten or overplayed clean part won't present problems or conflicts. This refers to sounds only. A useful comparison is that distorted sounds are thick, almost like a wall of sound, and clean sounds are clear and more bell-like. Here are examples of clean guitar parts.

1. Chord comping—rhythmic and sustained
2. Single-note, percussive, and rhythmic parts
3. Arpeggiation
4. Melodic fills
5. Solos
6. Fingerpicking

Artists and groups with typical clean guitar sounds include the following:

1. Andrés Segovia
2. Pat Metheney
3. George Benson
4. Wes Montgomery
5. Earl Kugh
6. Larry Carlton
7. Al McKay (Earth Wind, and Fire)
8. Jay Graydon (Al Jarreau)
9. Nile Rogers (David Bowie, Chic, Madonna, etc.)

Most R&B and pop records have clean guitar parts. They usually combine any or all of the following:

1. Sustained chords
2. Rhythmic comping (chords)
3. Single-note rhythmic parts
4. Melodic fills
5. Solos
6. Arpeggiation
7. Rhythmic and melodic ostinati that fit the chord progression

OTHER STYLES

Country music uses a wide variety of guitars or guitar-family instruments. The guitars usually predominate and are almost always clean, with electronic effects being used in subtle ways. Six- and twelve-string acoustic and electric guitars, pedal steel, banjo, and mandolin are frequently combined in groups on country records, with the keyboards in a support-pad role. There are country records that feature the keyboards, especially recent country-pop "hybrid" records. Some country and country-pop artists to listen to include the following:

1. Willie Nelson
2. Dolly Parton
3. Crystal Gayle
4. Mandrell Sisters
5. Kenny Rogers
6. O'Kanes
7. Glenn Campbell
8. Oak Ridge Boys
9. Ronnie Milsap
10. Dwight Yoakam

No discussion of guitar sounds or parts would be complete without mentioning some of the legendary jazz and blues artists. Among many things, these artists are masters of getting a wide range of sounds, expression, and vocal qualities from their instruments, with distorted and clean sounds. These artists and groups have an abundance of inflection and emotion:

1. Howlin' Wolf
2. B. B. King
3. Albert King
4. Muddy Waters
5. Robert Cray
6. Eric Clapton
7. Jimmy Page
8. Jeff Beck
9. Z. Z. Top
10. Django Reinhardt
11. Grant Green
12. Wes Montgomery
13. "Blind" Lemon Jefferson

Bluegrass and folk are the few remaining areas where acoustic guitar family instruments can still be heard. The instruments are picked with all the fingers, played with fingerpicks, or strummed. To hear some of the techniques and natural acoustic sounds of bluegrass and folk, listen to the following:

1. Bill Monroe
2. Earl Scruggs
3. Lester Flatt
4. Pete Seeger
5. Peter, Paul, and Mary
6. The Weavers
7. Joan Baez
8. Judy Collins
9. Woody Guthrie
10. Arlo Guthrie

GENERAL CONSIDERATIONS IN WRITING GUITAR PARTS

One of the primary differences between rock and R&B is that in rock the guitars are the focus, with the keyboards playing a secondary role. In R&B the guitars and keyboards roles are more evenly divided. When the keyboards are playing pads, the guitars are active and when the keyboards are active, the guitars play melodic fills, legato, sustained (pad), less rhythmically active, or lay out completely.

A fairly recent development that has affected the role of guitar is the presence of groups that blend R&B and rock approaches and sounds within a given arrangement. It used to be that rock was rock and R&B was R&B. The distinctions were very clear. In many cases that's still true. However, there are many top-forty pop-fusion groups that have successfully married elements of both styles. You tend to hear overdriven power chords accompanied by clean R&B-influenced rhythm parts. The following groups and artists are known to combine these different styles and sounds:

1. Robbie Neville
2. Mr. Mister
3. Toto
4. Culture Club
5. Genesis
6. Go West
7. Power Station
8. Robert Palmer
9. Thompson Twins
10. Sting—The Police
11. Level 42
12. Wang Chung
13. Scritti Politti

Studio guitarist Dave Lavender has these practical suggestions for playing and writing rhythm guitar parts:

On clean rhythm parts, try to imply the time, or groove by playing only what's necessary. Don't play every eighth- or sixteenth-note subdivision as a way of keeping time for yourself. Develop a well-defined part that has some breathing space in it. Don't get in the habit of tapping the strings constantly to keep the time; it ends up causing unneeded clutter. Concentrate on playing accurately and develop good time so you won't need that crutch.

If there are two or more guitar parts, they should be rhythmically independent, possibly in different registers and with different sounds. This lets each part contribute without clashing and also makes mixing much easier.

If the keyboard part is a pad or sustained part, I'll play more active rhythmically; when the keyboards are active, I go for a more legato or sustained part or play melodic fills and even lay out if I really can't add something significant.

In R&B, I tend to listen to the hi-hat part for the subdivisions and accents. This gives me something rhythmic to relate to and build a part around.

If I know that there is going to be more than one guitar part, I play my first part with the next one in mind. This way the breathing space or room is built in.

I'll deliberately avoid certain registers or rhythms if I know I'm going to overdub another part or someone else will be playing with me.

In recording and playing live, I try to get my effects to be integrated into the part so that they are one and the same. If the effects are part of the way I play a part, then it's best to record that way. Engineers like it, too. I hand them my cable and on the other end is the sound and part together. Certain R&B guitar parts require chorus, delay, compression, and noise gating to sound right, so I just get the whole routine together before tracking.

COMBINING GUITAR SOUNDS

Guitars are very flexible and are capable of blending with themselves in many ways. Here are some typical combinations you can try.

1. Double a power chord part with different effects on it. This can soften or spread out a power part.

2. Doubling a power part with a different overdriven sound. Vary the E.Q., pickups, amp or effect settings. In this way one can have maximum edge, the other will have body or thickness.

3. Play the same clean part with different effects. Use one group of effects (or none) on one part, and use another group of effects, or the same effects with different settings, on the other. This creates a very interesting and complex stereo guitar part. Don't overdo the effects; they tend to compound each other, and you risk loosing the pitch center and definition. Use the same guitar with different pickups or tone settings.

4. Use nonexact doubling. This happens when you play a slightly different version of the first part. The parts may be on different types of guitars, or use different sounds on the same guitar. Adding effects will obviate or minimize the differences.

5. Double guitar parts with nonguitar sounds, or double nonguitar sounds with guitars. Guitars are very effective in doubling keyboard and vocal parts. Before you double anything, ask yourself why. Doubling to create new layered sounds or to add power, color, or thickness works well. Doubling to cover a flaw or conceal a basic weakness in another part probably will end up compounding the problem, so fix the first part before you double. This is true for all instruments or sounds. George Benson's vocal-guitar solos are classic examples of interesting doubling. The word *doubling* should not be taken literally. The same or similar parts can be tripled or quadrupled. This is very common. Jay Graydon does it on Al Jarreau's albums, as do many rock and heavy-metal bands.

SPECIAL EFFECTS

1. *Feedback.* Controlled feedback is a part of many rock guitar solos. Feedback is produced by aiming the guitar's pickups directly at the amp's speakers. The amount of feedback is a function of the proximity of the guitar's pickups to the amp and the volume. Uncontrolled feedback is used for dramatic effects, but is harder to deal with once it's initiated. There are also effects boxes that simulate feedback. Listen to Jimi Hendrix, Van Halen, et al.

2. *Tremolo ("Whammy") bars.* These bars are attached to the bridge of the guitar and allow the player to bend all of the strings up, causing the pitch to bend sharp, or bend down, into the guitar, causing the pitch to go flat. The tremolo bar may be used for expressive or dramatic effects in solos. It is similar to the pitch bend function on synths.

One problem with the whammy bar is that it can wreak havoc with the guitar's overall intonation. One way to avoid this problem is to install a locking nut assembly on the guitar which, in effect, isolates the strings' intonation from the effects of the bar. Without this helpful device, the strings can suffer only so much stress and relief before they loosen up.

3. *Slide Guitar.* By placing a metal tube over one finger on the fretting hand and touching the tube lightly to the strings, a guitarist can produce sliding or glissando effects, and some other eerie effects as well. It's common to hear slide playing on pedal steel, traditional blues, and rock guitar parts.

4. *Harmonics.* Like any stringed instrument, the guitar has natural and artificial harmonics available on each string. They can be used in delicate passages, as well as for screaming high notes in overdriven rock solos. Harmonics are used more for effect than in the usual rhythm guitar parts. On electric guitars the volume of harmonics can equal that of regular notes.

5. *Signal Processing.* Effects boxes or studio outboard gear can cause subtle or radical changes to any guitar sound. Before adding any signal processing, it is a good rule of thumb to have a reason and a sound in mind. The most legitimate reason is in order to shape the sound to the part. Add one effect at a time so you can control the process of designing your sound. Understanding what each piece of equipment does will help you to write parts with sounds in mind, and it will also allow you to give more specific instructions to guitar players. Signal processing may add unwanted noise, and it is not unusual to have a noise gate as the last device in the signal flow before going into an amp or mixing console.

6. *Tuning.* The standard tuning for the guitar is almost always used, but by altering the tuning on any or all the strings some unusual effects are possible. A common pitch alteration is the use of a capo. This device clamps around the neck of the guitar and mechanically transposes the instrument. In effect it "shortens" the overall length of the neck, putting the whole guitar into a new key. As an arranger, you learn to be patient with certain guitarists' needs for frequent tuning adjustments. The intensity of playing, climate, and physical condition of the instrument are major factors in intonation. Most players have electronic tuners, so it should never be more than a momentary problem.

Encourage players to tune up frequently, especially if a critical part or take is coming up. Most players will automatically retune after any vigorous playing, but trust your ears, too. Avoid the mistakes before they happen. An ounce of prevention is worth a pound of cure.

CONCLUSION

The best ways to learn about guitar sounds and parts are by analytical listening and transcription and by spending as much time as you can with excellent players who will demonstrate the relationship between sounds and parts. Let them show you how the effects work and how instruments sound and function in different registers. If necessary, take some lessons even if you don't intend to play a note. Let a seasoned player or teacher guide you around the instrument. The guitar is a central instrument in all of today's music. The more you understand about the guitar, the more effectively you will communicate your ideas.

Working out Problems in the Rhythm Section

This really isn't that hard if you keep track of priorities and ask yourself the right questions. The number-one priority is a solid groove: All the sounds and parts must work well together rhythmically, harmonically, and melodically. All the parts contribute to the whole in such a way that nothing is distracting from the overall groove. There should be enough contrast between foreground and background. There should also be a few surprises or reinterpretations of common techniques, or different approaches to clichés to hold the listeners' attention.

Let's look at some specific problems that plague rhythm sections.

1. Too many similar parts in the same register.

2. Too much overall rhythmic activity. (Rhthym sections become cluttered and parts lack definition.

3. Not enough rhythmic activity overall. (Rhythm sections feel lethargic or empty.)

4. Good parts, but poor execution and sloppy performance.

5. Sounds are too thin or too dense for parts, or they are otherwise inappropriate.

6. Rhythmic conflict between parts. Syncopations are not uniform or complementary. Anticipations, delayed attacks, and downbeats conflict between parts.

7. Voicings or inversions of chords are not compatible between keyboards and guitars. Agreement needed on exact voicings.

8. Parts are poorly copied, layout is confusing. Beats, bars, and notes may be missing or unreadable.

9. Tempo is too fast or slow for parts to work. Alter tempo or rework the parts to fit existing tempo.

10. Stiff, rushed, or dragging feel. Discrepancies in the interpretation of time need to be worked out or parts reprogrammed with offsets or tempo variations.

11. Bass line and kick drum conflict rhythmically.

12. Intonation problems within a single instrument or among several.

13. Too many effects on sounds, causing loss of definition and pitch problems.

14. Sounds are too dry and need some effects.

15. Voicings are unbalanced, with too many big gaps, or they are muddy or thin.

16. Too many parts are doubled, causing sounds to be ineffectively thick or heavy. Rhythm section becomes bottom-heavy.

17. Not enough depth or warmth on bass and kick drum sounds. Bottom end sounds thin and anemic.

18. Sounds are too thick on bass or kick drum.

19. Drum kit sounds unbalanced. (For example, the snare is too loud or not loud enough, or overall sounds of drums are not compatible with each other.)

20. Drum parts are good, sounds are not working well on the parts, or drum parts need revision (too busy, too open).

21. Only one part is overactive, crowding everything else.

22. Only one part is underactive, leaving excessive rhythmic gaps.

23. Bass line doesn't agree with chord progression.

24. Harmonic or rhythmic conflict between guitars and keyboards or any other groups of instruments.

25. Problems in hearing other players or hearing yourself. Volume or mix-placement problems.

26. Personality conflicts

If you find a need to trouble shoot the rhythm section, try listening to parts in isolation, and then in any possible pairs, wherever you suspect a problem. Keep one part as a constant and play the others against it until you have found the culprit. This quickly isolates the problem. Happy hunting!

Chapter Ten ✍
Vocal Arranging

Writing for voices is similar to writing for instruments. The guidelines for solid musical thought apply, but there are some important musical, physical, and practical differences.

Unlike any other instrument, the sound of the voice is produced totally within the body. It's the only "living" instrument and is the one that all others imitate. Singers, much more than instrumental musicians, are expected to be entertainers. Without entering a discussion on values, there can be conflicts between music and entertainment. The incentives that society provides for becoming a singer are different from the incentives for becoming an instrumentalist, arranger, or songwriter.

Some singers regard themselves primarily as musicians and view their voices as instruments and as means of expression. For others, the entertainment aspects are more important than the music. There are those, however, who manage to do both extremely well.

For some singers, technique, or a lack of it, is a trademark. At one extreme is the singer with a lot of technique and no emotion. At the other extreme is a singer like Louis Armstrong, who had little or no technique and it really didn't matter. In this case, technique was a function of style.

From an arranging and technical point of view, there are two different groups of singers—those who are musically trained and those who aren't. This has nothing to do with talent, vocal ability, or creativity. As an arranger, you have to be able to work with both groups. This means communicating in the same musical language that you use with other trained musicians or modifying your approach and finding a common language for untrained singers. A singer with a great voice who can't read music may not understand a suggestion such as "sing the part up a minor third." You will probably have to help the singer find the notes if he or she can't hear them instinctively.

No matter what type of singers you work with, one of the most important aspects of your work is developing material that suits them emotionally and technically. Singers often have strong ideas about how they want songs arranged. You have to somehow absorb and digest that information and come up with an arrangement that satisfies their technical and emotional needs and the requirements of the job, as well as your needs.

This often requires the nonmusical skill of compromise, which is as valuable as any musical technique. An arranging assignment for singers can be regarded at this way:

Song	Arrangement	Singer
melody, lyrics, style, form, harmony (the basic ingredients)	style, form, harmony, key, sounds, parts, tempo, groove	male or female group, type of voice, range, qualities, style

Example 10.1 contains a list of the average male and female vocal ranges. Falsetto notes may extend beyond these ranges, but falsetto and its usefulness vary greatly from one singer to another.

The various writing options can be described by the following:

Melody 1:	Lead vocal	Solo (M or F)
		Group (M, F, mixed)
Options:	Unison double Octave unison double Harmony	
Melody 2:	Background vocals	Solo (M or F)
		Group (M, F, mixed)
Options:	Unison Octave Unison Harmony	

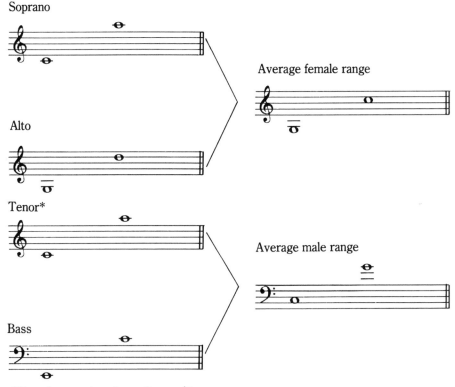

Soprano

Alto

Average female range

Tenor*

Average male range

Bass

*Sounds one octave lower than written

Example 10.1: Vocal ranges

Difficult intervals

major second   minor seventh   perfect fifth   perfect fourth   minor second   major seventh   tritone

Easy intervals

major third   minor sixth   minor third   major sixth

Example 10.2: Intervals for singers

Here's one example of how the above chart may be used. The lead (Melody 1) vocal is male, singing by himself; and the background vocals are a mixed male-female group, singing in harmony.

Under Melody 1, you can see one of the options as harmony. This means the melody can be sung in harmony. Don't confuse a harmonized lead vocal part with background vocals. Background vocals are a separate musical part, whether sung in unison or harmonized. This means that any line can be thickened in two ways—unison (octave unison) or harmony.

When you begin working with a singer or group of singers, there is preliminary information you will need to help you write effectively. This information will give you an opportunity to find a singer's

strengths and weaknesses early on in the writing process. It will also allow you to tailor the arrangement to the singer's personality. The information you get from this process will give you anything from general insights into a singer's character to ideas about how to write for a specific voice. Optimally, you will have heard the singer(s) before you begin working together. If not, try to get some tapes or see a performance. Here is a preliminary checklist to assist you in your work.

1. Learn the singer's range.

2. Learn the unique qualities of the voice, in all registers and at different volumes.

3. What notes or areas are especially strong or weak?

4. How flexible is the voice in terms of creating different colors in a given range? How well does it blend in a group?

5. Does the singer have any unique technical abilities, that is, scat-singing, wide range, special effects, or other languages?

6. Does the singer have any pitch, time, endurance problems?

7. Any physical problems that directly influence his or her abilities?

8. What are the singer's favorite types of music?

9. Who are the singer's biggest influences, favorite singers, musicians, arrangers, and producers?

10. Is there anything else you should know? What time of day or night does the voice sound best? (This is especially important if you are recording.)

These questions will help you write for a singer's strengths, minimize his or her weaknesses, and avoid writing "cloned" or generic arrangements.

Selecting the Right Key and Tempo

Once the material has been selected, the next issue is choosing the key and tempo. Choosing the right key is all-important for positioning the singer's voice in the strongest place for the technical and emotional demands of the song. The right tempo is critical in getting the maximum impact from the lyrics and phrasing.

ANALYZE THE MELODY

This will help you find the highpoints of a song, and will allow you to position the singer's voice in the strongest range. If the melody has an unusually wide range, you will be able to adjust the key so that you can minimize any awkward changes from one area of voice to another. You need to know where the singer's voice changes from chest to head (known as the *break*) and when it goes from full to falsetto. Choose a key that avoids switching voice placements at critical places in a melody. Watch out for transitions between sections, exposed entrances, the "big hook" of the song, or any extremes of vocal range or emotional expression. Poor choice of key can leave singers switching uncomfortably between chest and head voice or running out of range (high or low). Good choice of key positions the melody in such a way that entire phrases or sections can be sung in one area of the voice. Not every melody-singer combination will

allow this, so the next best thing to do is to position the melody so that the majority of notes in a phrase or section fall into one area of the voice. If the singers are patient, or have a sense of humor, try deliberately inappropriate keys so you can hear what the problems are firsthand. Don't count on all singers with the same general range to do things the same way. For example, not every female alto will switch from chest to head voice on the same note. Make few assumptions and work on a case by case basis. The voice is not like a trumpet in this respect. Some singers can make such smooth transitions from one part of their voice to another that you hardly notice them. Some singers have wider usable ranges than others.

PERFORMANCE

Another consideration in key selection has to do with live performance and order of songs. If you are arranging for a live situation where the singer is working almost every night and singing many songs in succession, then there are other considerations. Not every song should tax the singer's abilities, or use the extremes of their range. Consider the options of sometimes writing in lower keys to allow the singer to rest while singing.

Any given song may have several options for the choice of key. Consider the difficulty of the songs that come before and after the one you are working on. It's very common for pop singers to record a song in one key then lower the keys of some songs for long, hard tours.

MODULATIONS

If you are planning any modulations in an arrangement, determine the final key and work your way back. Working your way back from the end ensures that the singer doesn't wind up in an uncomfortable, or even worse, unsingable key. If you can determine the key with maximum impact for your last section, then it's easy to backtrack to the starting key. MIDI makes this particularly simple. Enter the chord progression into your sequencer and then transpose your keyboards. (Don't let MIDI prevent you from learning to play in all keys "the old way".)

TEMPO

Be sure that you choose a tempo that allows all the words to be sung comfortably. Find the most active part of the vocal and use this to adjust the tempo.

There are songs that seem to need slightly different tempos from section to section, so work this need into your programming or live rhythm section or try and find one tempo that works well throughout. Be sure the phrasing, breathing, and diction is comfortable—neither rushed nor dragging.

Live tempos are sometimes slightly faster than recorded versions of the same song. This is because the energy level in performance can give a natural edge to the time. This doesn't mean that it's okay to rush, however. Every rhythm section knows that glaring look received from a singer when the song was counted off too fast or too slow or the time picked up too much or started to drag. If you are responsible for count-offs, then sing the chorus (or any important section) in your head to the tempo before counting off. On a recording people listen with their ears only. In a live performance people also listen with their eyes. There is a lot more going on in a performance to distract the audiences attention of the audience from variations in tempo.

Unison Treatments

There are several ways to enhance lead or background vocals without adding harmony. When the details of a part have been worked out (for example, interpretations and phrasing), you can add a unison or octave-unison double. This is a matter of taste and should only be used when a thickened unison sound is desired. By using various types of signal processing, you can generate an artificial double in recording. This can be added to the live double. This technique adds a presence and fullness to a singer's voice. Be careful not to overwork the technique. Some lead vocals have the greatest power, intimacy, or honesty when left alone. Never double a part as a way of hiding flaws. The basic part must be strong; otherwise you create more problems than you solve. Doublings work well with the same or a different person doubling the part. Vocals that are very expressive, loosely phrased, or have lots of inflection and dynamics are difficult to double. They can also sound inappropriate when doubled. The urgency or honesty gets lost. Vocals sung without too much inflection or character are easier to double. Doubling also works well with group vocals, using any combination of unison or octaves. The most powerful effect often is a big unison sound. These doublings work well on lead and/or background parts. Table 10.1 presents the possibilities.

Doubling adds presence or emphasis to words or phrases without thickening the harmony. Again, don't consider unisons as last-resort options. Use them when and if effective.

TABLE 10.1
Unison Combinations.

Lead Vocal	Optional Background Vocals
M—solo	M—solo
F—solo	F—solo
M & F—unison	M & F—unison
M & F—octaves	M & F—octaves
M & M—unison	M & M—unison
M & M—octaves	M & M—octaves
F & F—unison	F & F—unison
F & F—octaves	F & F—octaves

Note:
Anything in the lead-vocal column can work with anything in the background column. (For example, Lead vocal = M & F octave unison; Background vocal = F & F unison.)

Vocal Harmony

Table 10.2 illustrates the possibilities for lead and background harmony in combinations. The same voicings work on lead or background parts.

TABLE 10.2.
Vocal Harmony Combinations.

Lead Vocal	Optional Background Vocals
solo	none
unison double	unison double
octave unison double	ocatve unison double
harmonized (one or more notes)	harmonized (one or more notes)
Possibilities for Harmony	*Possibilities for Harmony*
above melody (one or more notes)	(same as Lead Vocal)
below melody (one or more notes)	
above and below	
(one or more notes)	

The most common combination occurs when one part is in unison and the other can be harmonized. *Timbre* (quality, color) of vocals should be different from lead to background.

All voicing techniques used on acoustic instruments are technically possible. However, for the most effective or safest voicings, follow these guidelines: Use chord tones in close position; use tensions sparingly, with no seconds between the top two notes; and use smooth voice leading on all parts so that they move logically.

One big difference between the voice and other instruments is that the voice is an internal instrument and has no helpful keys or buttons to help establish and hold a pitch. Singers rely totally on their ears, sense of pitch, and vocal control. Everything associated with sound production, accuracy, and quality is internal. Microphones and amplification can be of tremendous help but only after the sound is produced internally.

Thirds and sixths are the safest intervals for vocal harmony. They are the easiest to hear, sing, and control. These intervals are also found most often in pop vocal harmony because the music is based on simple chords and voicings containing these intervals.

Avoid compound intervals (intervals over an octave in size). The spread between notes is too large to get a blend. Singing in tenths or elevenths is usually ineffective. Harmonies have more resonance when the voicings are more closely spaced.

The reason for avoiding seconds, sevenths, fourths, fifths, and compound intervals is simple. The word *interval* means distance, and these intervals are the hardest for average singer's ear to measure accurately. The pitches are therefore harder to control. Two or more people having similar problems makes the situation worse. Fourths or fifths are most effective when they are part of a triad or larger voicing because they are surrounded by easier intervals to sing. Fourths and fifths by themselves are hard to sing but are occasionally used for special effects.

Voicing Types

The same type of voicings will work on lead and background parts. A good rule of thumb is that when one part is voiced, the other will usually be unison. Harmony can be as simple as adding one new note to a part or as complex as voicing a full chord. Some of the most useful and common places for harmony are (1) harmony above melody; (2) harmony below melody; and (3) harmony above and below melody, with melody sandwiched between harmony (Example 10.3).

Example 10.3

When one harmony note is needed, try to find the nearest chord tone above or below the existing part. When two or more notes are needed, fill out the basic chord sound, in any of the three ways listed in the previous paragraph. Find a close position voicing, in any inversion, that contains a root, third, and fifth. Sevenths and well-supported tensions will occasionally be appropriate, depending on the style of music and ability of the singers (Example 10.4). If you do end up using tensions, the safest and most effective voicings are triadic. For example, if you have a C − 7 (11, 9) chord and want voices on tensions, voice the tensions as a close position B-flat triad (contains ♭7, 9, 11) (See Example 10.5.)

Example 10.4: Basic three-note chord sounds

These B triads provide the 7, 9, and 11 of the C minor.

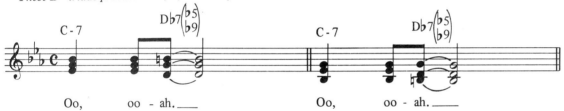

Example 10.5: Tensions using triadic voicings

Voicing techniques like drop two, drop two and four, drop three, and spreads are possible but sound best in the context of certain styles. These voicings are typical of traditional vocal groups, big bands, and jazz and pop-jazz vocal groups. Virtuoso vocal groups like Manhattan Transfer or Lambert, Hendricks, and Ross have musician-singers who have phenomenal control and ears. The vocal arranging can be much more involved harmonically, with voices treated like horns. Rich, dense, and varied voicings are possible with highly trained singers. This type of vocal writing is beyond the capabilities of most singers and requires a lot of rehearsal. (See Example 10.6.)

Developing Vocal Parts

Now that you have seen what types of intervals and voicings are most effective, analyze the lead vocal part for possible doublings or harmonies. There will be many occasions when you will want to develop additional independent parts.

Background vocals generally contain short phrases or motifs. They are normally not as developed as the lead vocal, in the same way that a counterline or secondary melody is not as developed as the

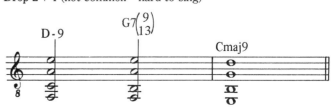

Example 10.6

Example 10.6 *(continued)*

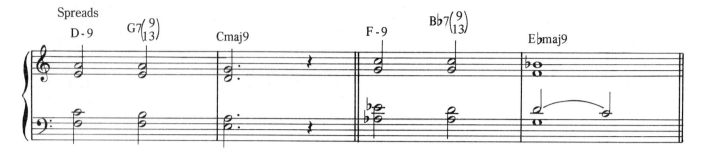

primary melody. (Since music is not an exact science, there are exceptions to this rule.) These are the options available to you:

1. Thicken the primary vocal (lead) by unison or adding harmony.

2. Create secondary background parts and perhaps thicken these with unisons or harmonies.

There are situations where the vocal is treated like a round or canon and several people are singing rhythmically displaced versions of the melody. (This is like a modern version of "Row, Row, Row Your Boat.") There are also situations where the background vocals (with their own identity) are as active and developed as the lead. This is akin to having two independent, contrasting lead lines or vocals. Earth, Wind, and Fire was famous for this technique.

Every style of music has its characteristic vocal harmonies, effects, and interpretations. The best way to learn about writing vocal parts in different styles is through analytical listening and transcription. Pick a few records in every style and study them. You will be surprised at how simple most vocal parts are. Very often blend, accuracy, conviction, energy, and intonation make the parts so effective. Vocal harmonies are similar to string voicings in that a very rich sound can be achieved with simple voicings, due to the natural potential for resonance.

Analyze a melody and be very conscious of its interpretation and phrasing. This will help you to build the additional vocal parts accurately. The interpretation and phrasing of the lead vocal contains vital information about how, when, and if you should thicken the lead vocal and guides you in writing background parts. The rhythmic entrances, style, phrasing, and interpretation of background vocals all depend on a complete understanding of the lead vocal.

In a recording situation it makes sense to get a definitive lead vocal before writing (or fine tuning) the backgrounds. The lead vocal interpretation will often give you ideas for background parts or for thickening the lead vocal.

In a performance situation let the lead vocalist become comfortable with the melody and lyrics before adding backgrounds. Even in top-forty copy bands, where a record is essentially copied, there may be room for individual reinterpretation of lead and background vocals.

There are many situations where everyone is singing the lead vocal for a phrase or section. This is common on choruses of pop songs. In these cases, you need to work out and agree upon the exact phrasings and interpretations, and stick to them; otherwise, the situations become free-for-alls.

To plan additional vocal parts, find the words or phrases that are already emphasized or that need emphasis. Look for high points, sustained notes, and accented or syncopated parts. In short, anything you want to emphasize or call attention to is a candidate. It may be a word or an entire phrase. You need to have a reason for adding or creating new parts. The reason should be that something in the vocal needs emphasis, or contrast. It's always easy to find spots for harmony. The real question is, does the music need it? Does the style in which you are writing imply certain kinds of parts or voicings?

Find the most important spots in a song for thickening or creating additional parts and work on those first. Ask yourself if the new parts add interest, or simply fill space. Don't be afraid to delete superfluous parts that don't genuinely add interest, emotion, or provide needed contrast. The vocals are the focus of an arrangement. If anything needs to be clear of distractions, they do.

The lyrics will suggest ideas for backgrounds. You can emphasize a thought in the lyrics by repeating a few words in a different way rhythmically, or you can use different vocal qualities in another register. Background vocals often become running commentaries on the main lyrics. The unison or voiced *oh-baby*s, *oh-yeah*s, and *uh-huh*s are like foils for the lead vocal to bounce off. They provide question and answer dialogues between lead and background vocals. These parts also help bridge or connect sections. It's common for short phrases to tie one area of an arrangement to another.

In general, background parts are made distinctive by any combination of the following elements:

1. Contrast in register

2. Contrast in timbre (different vocal quality)

3. Rhythmic contrast (opposite of lead vocal)

4. Rhythmic similarity (similar to or matches lead vocal, but timbre contrasts)

5. Attitude, energy, and articulation

6. Unison or harmony

7. Different lyric content

Vocal Blend

Vocal blend occurs in much the same way as instrumental blend. You need people whose voices are complementary and who have the desire to blend. The idea is to get a unified group sound where each individual voice becomes part of the group identity. This is a very different sound from a group of individuals singing together without blending.

Some singers are great for both solo lead vocals and group blending. However, there are those whose voices have such unique qualities that they really can't blend; no matter what they do, they can't neutralize those qualities to blend with a group. Finally, there are those whose voices are so neutral and adaptable that they really don't have enough unique qualities to be instantly recognizable as soloists.

Singers need to have well-constructed parts and voicings to blend. Use simple parts, close voicings, and chord tones to get the quickest and best results. Singers need to hear each other easily and must be physically close to create a blend.

Group vocals can involve any combination of male and female voices. A lot depends on the range of a part and whether you want perfect unisons, octaves, full voice, or falsetto. The best blend occurs when each singer is comfortable on his or her part, in an area of the voice that is easy to control and blend.

If the singer is relaxed and singing in a comfortable register, the sound will be relaxed. If you want an urgent or strained sound, make sure everyone sings in a register that allows them to do that.

Group vocals will have the sound of whatever voice predominates, male or female. In a group that has an equal number of male and female voices, the result is usually a group sound, that has a balanced quality. It's possible to have an equal number of male and female voices, yet one sound will predominate. This has to do with dynamics or intention to feature one over the other.

Balanced voicings usually have females singing adjacent notes (higher notes) and males singing their adjacent notes (lower notes). This gives singers a chance to support the other singers with similar vocal qualities in the same registers. You can experiment with alternating male and female note assignments, but the safest way is to use separate male and female

areas of a voicing. This technique produces the most uniform vocal qualities. As an example, the chords in Example 10.7 could be distributed in several ways, the most common of which have the two top notes sung by females and the two bottom notes sung by males. If you were using high tenors, or strong male falsetto singers, you could assign the top two notes of each chord to the male voices. The other two possibilities —alternating voices male-female-male-female or female-male-female-male—could prove useful, but you would still need male singers with fairly good high registers. If you find that any of the singers are uncomfortable or straining on a particular note, switch parts or try another inversion of the chord.

Example 10.7

Pitch

There are singers whose style, message and conviction are so compelling that we don't hear or care about pitch problems. The out-of-tune notes are incorporated into the style. While this may work for some, in most cases solid, accurate pitch is important. We spoke earlier about time and the fact that individual beats have a front, middle, and back. Pitch is very similar. Think of a note as being a circle that has a top, bottom and center of the pitch.

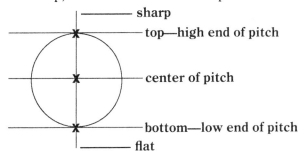

Anywhere in or on that circle can be considered to be in tune. Anywhere outside that circle is either sharp or flat. A lead or group vocal that is in tune has a centered, solid feeling. A vocal that is sharp or flat has a vaguely distracting, if not annoying, sound.

While some lead vocals may stray off pitch in moments of passion, group vocals can really fall apart if the pitch is not solid. Pitch problems in groups are compounded by the number of people. Group pitch is only as accurate as each individual's sense of pitch. Singers working in groups must first be confident about their own pitches. You can't expect someone else to hear pitch for you. When singers struggle to find their pitches and notes, blend is out of the question.

Vowel sounds or words that end with vowel sounds work well on repeated or sustained parts. Consonants do not sustain well due to their sounds and the way vocal chords and mouths work to produce those sounds. The most difficult consonants are the harsh "s," "c," and "z" sounds. These work best when released quickly or repeated quickly, as in

"ch-ch-cherry," "s-s-say," or "th-th-the." Vowel sounds work well on words or sounds like "ooo," "aah," "yeah," "hey," "nah," "no," and "woah." There are a few consonants that can sustain because the mouth is closed and doesn't need an abrupt or harsh cutoff. Examples are "mmmm" or "hummm." (See Example 10.8.)

Example 10.8: Vowels and consonants

Vibrato

There are as many kinds of vibrato as there are styles of music and individuals singing those styles. Vibrato is often very personal, and certain styles of singing have their own vibrato signatures or trademarks. There are some specific guidelines about using vibrato.

1. On a lead vocal vibrato can be a very important part of personal expression, adding intensity and emotion. However, a little bit usually goes a long way. A mixture of straight tone and vibrato is most common. Vibrato is used to color, taper off, or emphasize important or sustained notes.

2. The speed and depth of vibrato on vocals is very personal but is also a function of the tempo and style of the music.

3. Vibrato plus inflections give extra interest and character to important notes or phrases. This is a common way of punctuating or emphasizing a word or phrase.

4. In group vocals, either lead or background, the use of vibrato becomes critical. If vibrato is used, it must be worked out. Group vocals need to match vibrato characteristics (speed and depth) and plan when to use vibrato. Group vocals without vibrato tend to have a certain fullness just from the natural "chorusing" of the voices. Use of vibrato in group vocals can be effective to emphasize or

shade important notes or to end sustained notes naturally. This must be planned to avoid pitch or blend problems. If you are in doubt, use this technique sparingly.

5. Vibrato should never be used to mask pitch problems or insecurities about what to do with exposed or sustained notes. Vibrato is only beautiful if it is placed on a strong and in-tune note. Good pitch, breath support, and solid execution come first. Vibrato is an important effect; it should never replace what should be at the foundation. Vibrato placed on inaccurate pitch or done with sloppy execution is like adding insult to injury, and most listeners can tell something is wrong.

Falsetto

A useful analogy for describing falsetto is putting a capo on a guitar. Not all singers have a falsetto voice, and those that do have many different qualities and ranges. There is no absolute rule in using or avoiding falsetto, except that you must use it carefully and on an individual basis. It can be useful and powerful or overpowering and annoying. A common use for falsetto is to have a male tenor sing falsetto in unison with a female. The usefulness of this depends on the quality and control of each singer. Many high parts become possible when singers (solo or group) have falsettos.

Dynamics

As with any instrument or group of instruments, dynamics are relative. Six females singing a high falsetto part marked fortissimo will be much louder than a solo tenor singing fortissimo in the middle of his range. Consider the effect you want, the range of the part, and the number of people on each note when you write the dynamics. Communicate to the singers by writing important instructions on their parts. For example, vocal group: mp (lead vocal soft here). Let the singers know what is happening in the other parts.

Using Voices as Instruments

Singers with well-developed senses of pitch and rhythm can use their voices to imitate or simulate instrumental sounds and parts. This usually involves using syllables that allow the voice to match the sounds and inflections of other instruments. It works well as a vocal part, ad-lib solo, and is very effective in doubling existing parts. For example, you can use voices to double a horn part or horn-section soli.

Female voices can be used to double or sing additional trumpet parts. Try scat-singing a part to see what syllables fit the style, rhythms, articulations, and tempo. You can do interesting imitative things with human voices. Try having a group of female voices use a vibrato that imitates an organ's spinning Leslie speaker. The possibilities for experimentation are endless. Again, it will help you to have a reason for doing what you do. Having a particular effect or sound in mind will guide you. Al Jarreau; Bobby McFerrin; Manhattan Transfer; Lambert, Hendricks, and Ross; and Eddie Jefferson are a few of the great artists who use their voices in this way.

Voices can be used to thicken any other nonvocal parts in an arrangement. This can be very dramatic or subtle. Assign the vocals to all or part of the instrumental voicing or unison line. Choose syllables that deliberately blend or contrast with the sounds to get the desired effect. Guitar and keyboard pad parts can be reinforced with vocal doubling. Rhythmic parts also work well. This technique requires patience, experimentation, and enough of the right voices. It is not a gimmick, and it can be as powerful as any other technique. (See Example 10.9.)

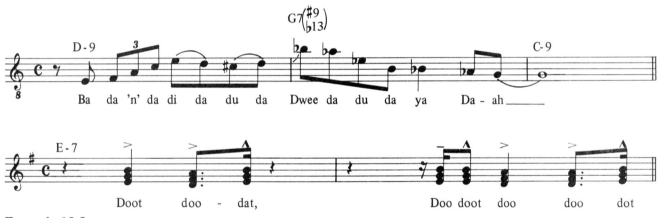

Example 10.9

Live, Recording, and Rehearsal Techniques

No matter where singers are, they must be able to hear themselves easily. They also need to hear any other part that influences their part in a critical way (time, pitch, or phrasing).

EFFECTS

It's best to leave any radical signal processing off the basic keyboards and guitars (chorus, flange, and delay) when vocalists are learning their parts or when they are recording parts that require a stable pitch reference. Singers rely on fixed pitch instruments to

lock in on their pitches. If the keyboard pad is heavily chorused at a vocal rehearsal or recording, it may create pitch problems. Those effects that spread out the pitch center beautifully can also wreak havoc on singers' pitch when they are just getting comfortable with the music.

PARTS

Vocal parts (for those singers who read music) should be as neatly and accurately copied as any other parts. Cue in any useful hints or lines from other parts that will help them locate where they are. If singers have many measures or rest before they enter, cue a few notes or words from other parts to help lead them in. It will be appreciated. Vocal parts can be copied out individually or each singer can have a copy of a master vocal part and learn his or her individual notes from it. On complicated or active music, each singer should ideally have his or her individual part. Appoint someone as the leader for giving cues, cutoffs, entrances, and dynamics. This really helps tighten the group sound and avoids unnecessary guesswork.

PERFORMANCE VOLUME

A good cue mix in recording or a separate vocal mix on stage makes a huge difference in vocal performance. It doesn't matter how good or loud the vocals sound somewhere else, if the singers are uncomfortable in any way, that will always influence their performances.

The fact that someone else can turn a singer's mic up or down is important, but don't enter into volume wars where there are no winners. Singers can't "turn up" their vocal chords as an amp can. The balance and sound quality must happen before the amplification. The best live and recorded vocal blends happen when singers can always hear themselves and other critical parts easily, and at comfortable volumes. When singers have to sing louder than is natural or comfortable for a part, the first thing to suffer is pitch. Acoustic instruments (including vocals) can be played or sung only so loudly before the pitch loses its center. If everyone can hear comfortably, someone else can turn up the house or control-room volume and it won't matter to the performers.

EMOTION AND TECHNIQUE

The ideal performance is technically and emotionally strong. The flaws are few, if any. This is what everyone looks for. In reality, some performances lack in one area or the other. In a live situation, it's a one-shot deal. You get what you get. In recording, the obsessive pursuit of a "perfect" vocal usually ruins any chance of spontaneity or emotion. Not many people can stay excited over a lyric for too long. A good rule of thumb for lead vocals is to get the best performance you can in three or four takes and move on. If it doesn't happen, come back to it later. If in those first few takes you have the basis of an emotionally strong and technically acceptable track, fix the small details right there, when you have that specific vocal quality. Trying to punch in random words or phrases on different days is risky. The vocal quality may not match up, and then you will have to redo the whole thing anyway.

If you are forced to make a choice between emotion and technique, take emotion. In the final analysis, people respond to conviction more than, for example, flawless pitch. There are many legendary performances to support this. you ultimately hope to get it all—emotion and technique.

Background vocals are not always as vulnerable as lead vocals. You can spend more time in your pursuit of perfection on background parts. Background vocals need plenty of attitude and energy to be convincing, but by their definition, they don't usually sustain the emotion for as long as the lead can. They often have longer rests between phrases to get "psyched up." Technically strong backgrounds can be built a little more methodically than lead vocals. Experienced and flexible singers will usually have more concentration and endurance for multiple takes on backgrounds.

RECORDING AND REHEARSING VOCAL HARMONIES

When you record harmonies one part at a time, the easiest and most logical way is to begin with the bottom note and work your way up. This allows subsequent parts to have a solid reference point by establishing a foundation. In this way you can be sure that each note is strong before moving up the chord.

It is very common to record each harmony note with several voices on it. This way everyone sings in unison and reinforces each note. As you overdub, it may make you more comfortable to pan the previous part(s) to one side and hear the part you are singing now panned to the opposite side. This prevents things from getting bogged down in the center.

Another technique is to record with one ear of the headphones on and the other off. This allows you to hear yourself and the other singers "live" in the room and allows a natural blend. Be sure the instruments or voices that serve as pitch references do not have unnecessary effects that diffuse the center of the pitch. Too much reverb can wash out the center of pitch.

Voices should sound natural. If they do, it's easier to get a good performance. Earlier we mentioned that effects are often integral to instrumental parts, but vocals are one area where you should try to save the effects for the mix. This is because (1) singers are most comfortable and accurate when there are a minimum of things to deal with during a performance; and (2) vocals are the most noticeable element of a recording, so you want to allow for as many mixing options as possible by recording "dry." Singers need to hear (monitor) themselves with some natural ambience (reverb). Try not to print the reverb on tape until you mix. For those people working in small or home studios, if you need to print the vocals with effects, become completely familiar with the parts so you can select the most appropriate effects.

DIFFICULT VOICINGS

One way to make recording a difficult vocal voicing easier is by recording the voicing one note at a time. Have everyone sing the same note. (Be sure it's strong and in tune.) Once that note is safely on tape, have everyone sing the next but keep the first note out of their headphone mix. They will sing each note as if it were the first. Proceed this way, with the singers hearing only the present note, until the voicing is complete. Now you can play back all the parts and the voicing should sound full and slick, without too much trouble. This is obviously a technique for recording only. The singers can get each subsequent pitch into their ears between takes by using a nearby keyboard for reference. (See Example 10.10.) Be sure to be extra conscious of entrances and cutoffs, since you won't be hearing the other parts. Listen for and use cues in the music or work with a click track.

There are certain other techniques that are very effective in vocal writing. They require some rehearsal but are not too difficult. Example 10.11 illustrates some useful techniques.

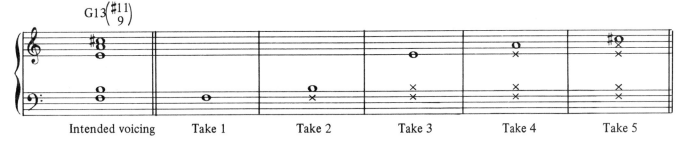

Example 10.10 *Recording a difficult vocal voicing*

Exaggerated dynamics

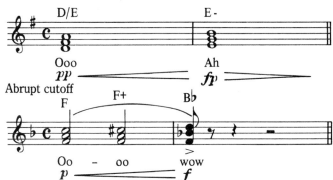

Some voices cut off while one voice continues (usually lead vocal, often ad lib)

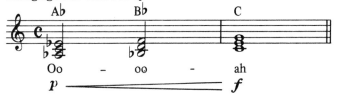

Changing from closed to open vowel sounds as volume increases

Rhythmic/percussive vocal writing

Example 10.11: *Some useful vocal writing techniques*

CHAPTER ELEVEN ✍
TRANSCRIPTION TECHNIQUES

Throughout this book we have consistently referred to the value of transcription as a tool for developing arranging skills. One of the best ways to learn how things are put together is to take them apart and see how the individual parts work and how they relate to each other and the whole. Taking a few "licks" off a record involves transcription techniques but teaches nothing unless the concept behind the part is understood. The goal of transcription should be to understand the concept that creates the part. In addition to transcribing parts, we need to ask ourselves the questions that reveal the underlying concepts. Things happen for reasons, and they are what we are after. The parts we hear are manifestations of ideas or concepts. The following questions will help you understand the concepts behind parts.

1. What is the purpose of this part? What role does it play in the music?

2. How does the part relate to the others and to the whole?

3. How would I describe this part in musical and aesthetic terms?

4. What is the person who wrote or played the part trying to accomplish? Why is the part in a particular octave, and why it is active, inactive, and so forth?

5. Is the part effective, and is it doing what was intended?

6. Do I understand the concept and the nature of the part well enough to create similar parts of my own?

By thinking through questions like these and by understanding the concepts, you will be able to go beyond imitation to creation of your own parts.

Improving Your Listening Abilities

Transcription involves listening to and analyzing parts in isolation. Concentrate initially on transcribing one part at a time. After a while you may be able to isolate several parts at once, and notate them. Transcription requires that you develop your powers of concentration to a high degree. Music is the kind of discipline that easily becomes all-consuming. To transcribe accurately and understand the concept, you need your full attention focused on the task at hand. Being patient and relaxed will allow you to be more effective. The skills come slowly but steadily, so don't waste precious time and energy getting angry at yourself if you can't notate something right away. If your ears are a little rusty or need more basic training, here's a list of suggestions to make your transcription work easier. (Practice with a friend, taking turns at the keyboard.)

1. *Learn solfège* (movable "doh"). This means the root-tonic is "doh" in whatever key your are in. Example 11.1 shows the syllables for movable-doh solfège in major and minor keys.

2. *Learn to identify what note of a chord is in the melody.* Every chord tone and tension has its own unique sound, character, or color. Have someone play increasingly more complex chords and practice identifying which note is on top of the voicing. Start with triads and add sevenths, ninths, elevenths, and thirteenths.

3. *Interval recognition.* Have someone play intervals within a given octave as well as compound intervals (larger than an octave). Practice identifying them melodically (one note at a time) and harmonically (both notes sounding together).

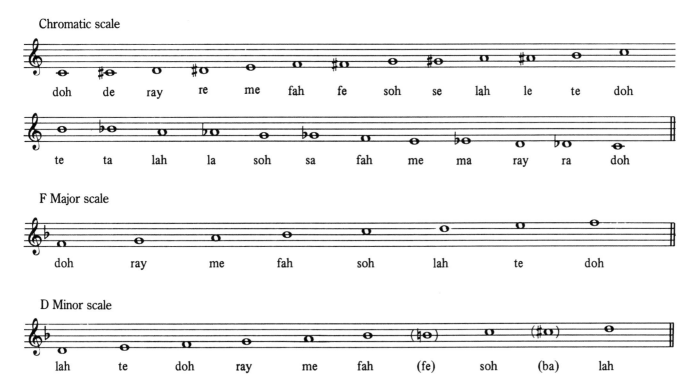

Chromatic scale

doh de ray re me fah fe soh se lah le te doh

te ta lah la soh sa fah me ma ray ra doh

F Major scale

doh ray me fah soh lah te doh

D Minor scale

lah te doh ray me fah (fe) soh (ba) lah

Example 11.1: Solfège—moveable do

4. *Harmonic Dictation.* Have someone tell you what key you are in and give you the I chord (tonic). Then have that person play simple, short chord progressions. Write them down away from any instrument. Increase the length and complexity of the progressions. Start diatonically and then gradually expand the harmonies. Every interval, chord type, and voicing has its own signature sound or identity. Learn to recognize chords by their telltale sounds. Association will help you with this process. You probably recognize intervals or chords from various pieces of music. Use that association to help implant the characteristic sounds in your ears. Start with intervals and add chord tones and tensions.

5. *Melodic Dictation.* Have someone give you the key and starting note and play increasingly longer and more complex melodies. Start diatonically and

add chromatic notes. Write out the melodies away from instrument.

6. *Rhythmic dictation.* Have someone tap or play increasingly longer and more syncopated rhythms. Use a metronome or click. Also learn to transcribe drum machine patterns. Start simply and increase the number of drum voices, the complexity and the length of patterns. Subdividing is the key to accurate rhythmic dictation. If you are having trouble with a rhythm, try this procedure. Determine the smallest unit of subdivision and write out as many bars of that subdivision as the phrase is long. find out which of the subdivisions the rhythm falls on. Remember that downbeats will feel more stable than offbeats or syncopations. Most subdivisions in pop music are quarter, eighth, or sixteenth notes with occasional thirty-second notes. (Example 11.2)

Original rhythm

Eighth-note subdivision

Example 11.2

Original rhythm

Sixteenth-note subdivision

General Suggestions

If you need to slow the tempo down, consider singing the part, if not in the exact pitches, then in the rhythms. Try to hear parts in phrases. first get a picture of the phrase structure before working on the minute details. Trying to transcribe a part note by note before you understand the larger context is like driving a car while looking right in front of the hood. While you work on the details, you also need to see or hear where you are going. If you can't get a clear picture of the phrase, slow it down, but still try to understand the entire phrase first. Always keep the subdivisions going in reference to a click or a drum machine. If your own time is strong, you will be able to count and subdivide accurately in your head as well as out loud. From working with a click, your internal time clock will eventually become quite accurate.

Before transcribing any part, try to characterize it. find some way of describing it accurately in musical terms. Let's say you are about to transcribe a difficult bass line. You might first describe it this way: In the synth bass, the range is an octave (approximately); the part is highly syncopated (sixteenth notes); there are many rests; the notes are tied across bar lines (watch out!); and the part is mainly roots, but there are other notes such as passing tones. Once you have learned to characterize accurately, it soon becomes a reflex. You will find yourself instantly assessing the part, recognizing the difficult areas, and quickly transcribing it. After you have done a fair amount of transcription in various styles, most parts you hear will be combinations or variations of parts you already know. Transcription is cumulative. It gets easier as you build up your recognition skills and musical vocabulary.

Try to transcribe away from your instrument. Use it to get the starting pitch only. This builds technique and confidence, even if the going is slow at first. Plunking away one note at a time does more harm than good. Your ears and confidence never develop because they are being led around, hearing after the fact. Use the keyboard only to verify your work; this way your ears are leading. It may be slow at first, but ultimately it is the way your ears grow. Otherwise, there are serious limitations on your development.

Let your mind help your ears. The process of elimination can help you out of a jam. For example, let's say you can hear that an interval in a melody is smaller than a fifth but bigger than a second. Let the process of elimination help narrow your choices. Your intellect and ears must work together as a team, zeroing in on the final note. If you understand something intellectually before hearing it, let your mind guide you, by elimination from the general to the specific.

Put the section of music you are working with on tape, if it isn't already. Use the vari-speed function on particularly active or complex parts. Combinations of vari-speed and E.Q. can help isolate parts for easier access. Try to "zero in" on the frequency with your E.Q. and tone controls. This can help lift the part out of context.

RHYTHMIC TRANSCRIPTION

Any musical part will have a rhythm. If it is also melodic or harmonic, you may be more comfortable dealing with one element at a time. The most basic element is rhythm, so start with that. Use subdivisions to help transcribe the rhythm, then fill in the notes, harmony, and so forth. Block out the number of bars on music paper. Indicate any particularly tricky or unusual areas by marking (*) on that bar or in the general area of the bar.

BASS LINES

Bass lines and kick drum are usually the lowest pitches on a pop record, and their parts are related. Use one to help you hear the other. Experiment with the tone controls (E.Q.) on your equipment to highlight the bass part. If you can't get the notes and rhythms simultaneously, get the rhythms first and then fill in the notes. Characterize the part: syncopated, straight, busy, ties over bar lines, closely related (or not) to kick drum, ostinato, pedal, or accents. Don't worry too much about thumb snaps and embellishments at first. Get the substance of the part, and later you can add the slick fills. Use a click and subdivide. You may want to speed the tape up or down to highlight the bass line. Determine if the bass part is harmonic (root-oriented) or melodic (roots plus a more developed melodic shape). Is the bass note a root or some other note?

MELODIC TRANSCRIPTION

The two components in melodic transcriptions are notes and rhythm. On particularly tricky melodies, transcribe the rhythm first. Examine the melody and characterize it. What is the range? Sing it and make note of any difficult intervals. Draw its curve or general shape. Does the melody move by steps, skips, or both? On long melodies work phrase by phrase. Lay out the entire number of bars first; then fill them in phrase by phrase. If your ears are well developed and the melody isn't ridiculously hard, you should be able to write it out (away from any instrument) once you have the starting pitch.

HARMONIC TRANSCRIPTION

There are four things to consider when transcribing chord progressions.

1. Root/note in bass

2. Chord type (major, minor, or V7 ♭9)

3. Voicing type (fourths, clusters, or triads)

4. Harmonic rhythm (rhythm in which chords move —sustained or syncopated)

If the chord progression is particularly difficult, you may need to work on one element at a time. For the purpose of this technique, the root/bass note does not have to be the actual bass line; it can be the one note to which the rest of the chord belongs. Try to identify the chords and types of voicings by their characteristic sounds. Harmony can be described as structures over roots (bass notes).

Structures (Chords and Voicings)

ROOTS/BASS NOTES

Ask yourself what note is in the bass. Is it a root or another note diatonic to the structure above it (for example, C, C/E, C/G)? Is the note in the bass not diatonic to the structure above it (for example, G♯/G)? Every chord-voicing combination has a unique sound associated with it. Is the structure a triad, a seventh chord? How is that structure voiced?

Relate the structure to the bass note. This is the note that tells you about the nature (major, minor) of the chord. For example, an F triad is a major triad

with an F as the bass note (root). An F triad with D in the bass is not F/D, it is D−7. The same upper structure will have a totally different sound when you change bass notes. Always relate the structure to the bass note and vice versa.

Let the process of elimination help you. If you are stuck on a particular chord, ask yourself some questions. Is it major or minor, a triad, a seventh chord, or larger? Does it have tensions, and if so, what kind? Sing the top note of the voicing and relate it to the bass note. Is it a chord tone, a tension, or a passing tone? What kind of voicing is it? Close, spread, fourths? Is the basic sound of the structure triadic, but is it over a bass note that creates more tension than a diatonic bass note (for example, F/B)? Is the note in the bass the root? If not, what function of the root is it? Are the chords moving over a pedal or ostinato? (This definitely has a unique sound, with more tension.)

The primary identity of a chord comes from the root and third. Try to hear that relationship first, then listen for the 5, 7, 9, 11, 13, and so forth. Practice playing and hearing all types of chords from triads on up, in any inversion or voicing. Do this in all keys. You probably associate certain chords and voicings with different pieces of music. Let this help in your transcriptions.

In pop music there are so many chords that you will re-encounter. The voicing types will vary more. No matter how a chord is voiced, it usually has a root and a third. This should always be your first point of reference. Your ears and the process of elimination can quickly fill in the remaining notes. Voicings in fourths or add2 chords often have no thirds, and their telltale sounds will alert your ears.

Conclusions

Begin transcribing music that is well recorded and has relatively simple, well-defined parts. Work in as many styles as you can, and choose examples that are very characteristic of a particular style. Work on one element at a time. It's not always necessary to transcribe an entire part. Get enough of the part to really understand the concept. Usually eight or sixteen measures will contain all or most of the vital information you need. Transcribe drum parts, percussion, rhythmic and sustained parts, melodies, counterlines, and horn parts. Write down your ideas about the parts. Try to come to some conclusions about how and why these parts were developed. Use these as role models for your own work, now that you understand the concept behind the part. Write the parts out neatly and accurately with dynamics, articulation, and comments, or store them in your sequencer. Be sure to describe the sounds, orchestration, and instruments.

Working with headphones can be helpful in bringing a particular part to your attention. Be careful to rest your ears periodically, and watch the volume. Audio fatigue can set in quickly with headphones. You will tend to ignore this when lost in the maze of transcribing difficult parts. Working with tired ears really doesn't yield accurate results. Remind yourself to rest for a minute. You will return refreshed and possibly with a new perspective on how to understand the problem at hand. Transcription can be tedious. Avoid extra confusion by working neatly. When you are done, the final version should be well documented and in one place rather than scattered among several pieces of paper or areas of your sequencer.

CHAPTER TWELVE
USEFUL CHARTS, TABLES, AND CHECKLISTS

This chapter contains references, definitions, charts and layouts that are useful in any arranging project. They will save time while helping you communicate clearly and effectively.

There are universal symbols for shortcuts in scoring and writing parts. The symbols have Italian names, but we will define them in English. They are used to save time and paper, and your players will immediately understand them. (Examples 12.1 through 12.4 show how these appear on music paper.)

1. *D. 𝄋 :* go back to the sign (𝄋).

2. *D 𝄋 al Fine:* go back to the sign (𝄋) and proceed to wherever you see the word "Fine" (end). This may appear anywhere in the music.

3. D 𝄋 al ⊕: go back to the sign (𝄋) and proceed until you see a (⊕) symbol, then skip to the part of the music marked (⊕).

4. ⊕ : indicates the coda section of a piece of music. It is usually found at the end.

5. *D.C.:* go back to the beginning.

6. *D.C. al Fine:* go back to the beginning and stop at the word "Fine."

7. *D.C. al⊕:* Go to the very beginning until you see the coda (⊕) sign and skip to the coda (⊕) section. Any of instructions (1–7) may also contain an additional marking to indicate which ending to use on the D 𝄋 or D.C. For example, D 𝄋 (second ending) al ⊕ means to take the D 𝄋, use the second ending, and go to the coda.

8. 𝄇 : A common musicians' "slang" marking. The eyeglasses mean to pay extra attention to the area marked. Usually the glasses are placed above the area. Arrangers and players indicate this on difficult parts.

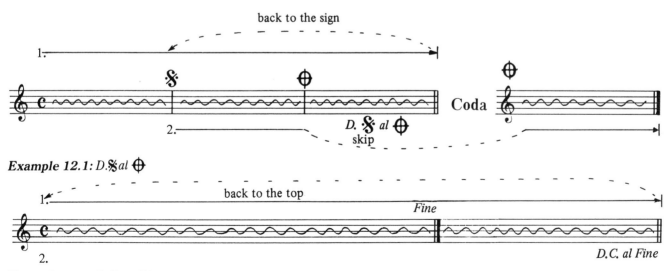

Example 12.1: *D.𝄋al ⊕*

Example 12.2: *D.C. al Fine*

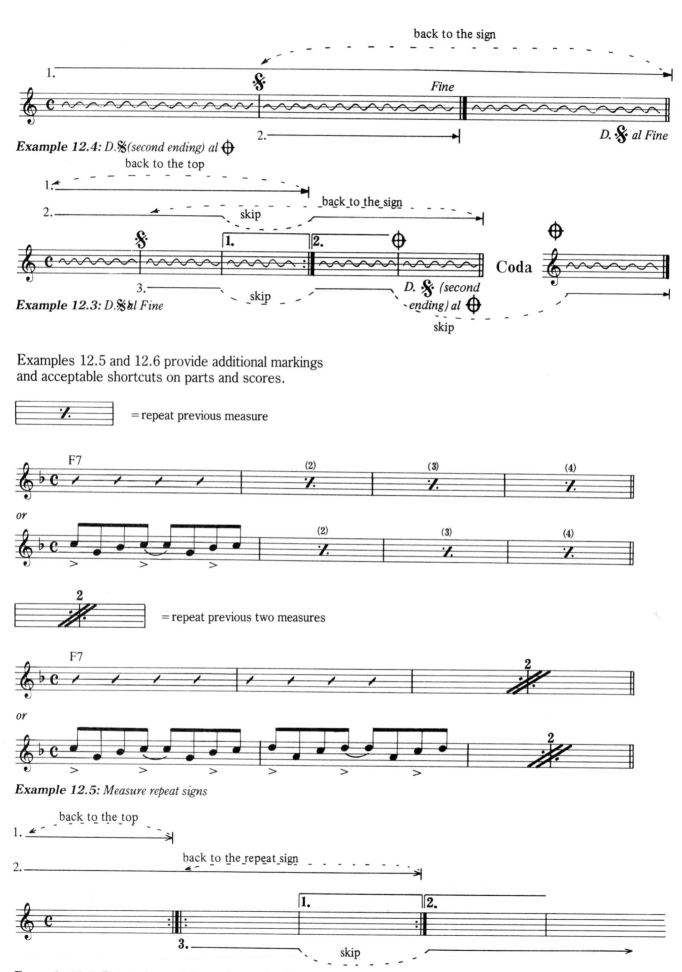

Example 12.4: *D.$\%$(second ending) al ⊕*

Example 12.3: *D.$\%$al Fine*

Examples 12.5 and 12.6 provide additional markings and acceptable shortcuts on parts and scores.

= repeat previous measure

= repeat previous two measures

Example 12.5: *Measure repeat signs*

Example 12.6: *Repeat signs and first and second endings*

Example 12.7 shows dynamic markings (relative volume and intensity). Any dynamic marking will remain in effect until a new marking takes its place.

Soft

ppp = *pianississimo*—extremely soft

pp = *pianissimo*—very soft

p = *piano*—soft

mp = *mezzo piano*—medium soft

mf = *mezzo forte*—medium loud

f = *forte*—loud

ff = *fortissimo*—very loud

fff = *fortississimo*—extremely loud

Loud

◁ or *cresc.*- - - - - - - - = *crescendo*—gradually getting louder

▷ or *dim.*- - - - - - - - = *diminuendo*—gradually getting softer

Example 12.7: *Dynamic markings*

8va ⌐ ⌐ or *8* ⌐ ⌐ ⌐ ⌐ = *ottava*—play one octave higher (used only above treble clef passages)

15ma ⌐ ⌐ or *15* ⌐ ⌐ ⌐ = *quindicesima*—play two octaves higher (used only above treble clef passages)

8va - - ⌐ or *8* - - - ⌐ = *ottava bassa*—play one octave lower (used only below bass clef passages)

15ma - ⌐ or *15* - - ⌐ = *quindicesima bassa*—play two octaves lower (used only below bass clef passages)

⌒ = *fermata*—hold note(s) or rest, continue on cue

❜ = *breath*—short pause

// = *pause*—break or stop in the music, continue on cue

Example 12.8: *Transposition and miscellaneous markings*

Example 12.9 shows correct notation of triplets.

Example 12.9: *Correct notation of triplets*

The following is a list of essentials on any part or score:

1. clef(s)

2. key signature

3. time signature

4. tempo marking or bpm (for example,   = 108)

5. dynamics

6. rehearsal letters

7. articulations

8. phrasing marks

9. correct form instructions: repeats; D , D.C.,   ; first and second endings.

10. any useful instructions or cues

11. special tempo instructions, holds, cutoffs, ritards, or accelerandos

Example 12.10 gives a "generic" part, with examples of the necessary markings, indications, and special instructions.

Example 12.10

Frequently Used Musical Terms

a capella: unaccompanied. (For example, you may ask the lead vocalist to sing the part *a capella.*)

accelerando: increase in tempo, gradual or rapid.

accidental: occasional sharps or flats not in key signature (only pertains to the note within the bar or if tied across a bar).

ad lib: improvise.

a tempo: return to the original tempo after a departure (slower or faster).

beats (in acoustics): These result from the interference of two sound waves of very similar, but not identical, frequencies. You will hear beats when two instruments play a unison note but not quite in tune. The beats disappear if the instruments are perfectly in tune.

col.: play with. As in *col. trumpet,* or *col. TRPT 8vb. Col.* is always followed by another instrument's name.

concert (concert pitch): Nontransposed, absolute pitch.

diatonic: pertaining exclusively to the notes in a given key or scale.

downbeat: the actual beats in a measure, not the subdivisions.

loco: back to original part.

poco a poco: little by little, slowly, as in *accel. poco a poco* (getting faster little by little).

ritardando (ritard, rit.): slowing down.

rallentando (rall.): same as rit.

rubato: take liberties with the time, expanding or compressing the rhythmic values of the notes.

segue: continue directly to next section.

simile: play in the same way as previous indications on score or part.

tacet: silent. A part previously played may later be marked *tacet.* At this point, don't play.

tonality: refers to the key center or the fundamental from which melody and harmony originate.

vamp: repeat of a certain section. Vamps are often marked *vamp and fade* on recording parts or *vamp until cue,* which means keep playing the section until given a cue to move on.

V.S. (volti subito): literally, "turn the page quickly"— used in parts as a warning to the player of an awkward page turn or to indicate that the piece continues on the next page if there could be some confusion.

TABLE 12.1.

Tempo Conversion Chart

bpm (beats per minute)	measures in 60 seconds		number of beats in:		
	$\frac{4}{4}$	$\frac{3}{4}$	30 seconds	20 seconds	10 seconds
60	15	20	30	20	10
63	15¾	21	31½	21	10½
66	16½	22	33	22	11
69	17¼	23	34	23	11½
72	18	24	36	24	12
76	19	25⅓	38	25⅓	12⅔
80	20	26⅔	40	26⅔	13⅓
84	21	28	42	28	14
88	22	29⅓	44	29⅓	14⅔
92	23	30⅔	46	30⅔	15⅓
96	24	32	48	32	16
100	25	33⅓	50	33⅓	16⅔
104	26	34⅔	52	34⅔	17⅓
108	27	36	54	36	18
112	28	37⅓	56	37⅓	18⅔
116	29	38⅔	58	38⅔	19⅓
120	30	40	60	40	20
126	31½	42	63	42	21
132	33	44	66	44	22
138	34½	46	69	46	23
144	36	48	72	48	24
152	38	50⅔	76	50⅔	25⅓
160	40	53⅓	80	53⅓	26⅔
168	42	56	84	56	27
176	44	58⅔	88	58⅔	29⅓
184	46	61⅓	92	61⅓	30⅔
192	48	64	96	64	32
200	50	66⅔	100	66⅔	33⅓
208	52	69⅓	104	69⅓	34⅔

Table 12.1 shows how to convert bpm to measures or number of beats in ten-second, twenty-second, and thirty-second amounts. This is useful when you want to know how long a piece of music will be at a given tempo or what tempo to use with a given number of measures. It comes in handy for underscoring, commercials, and any application where exact timings are critical. Simple math and a calculator will give you the same results, but this table illustrates some of the more common tempos.

Here's how to use the conversion chart in Table 12.1. Let's take the bpm setting of 112 for the purposes of illustration.

At 112 bpm in $\frac{4}{4}$, there are 28 measures (112 ÷ 4 = 28).

At 112 bpm in $\frac{3}{4}$, there are 37⅓ measures (112 ÷ 3 = 37⅓).

At 112 bpm, there are 56 beats in 30 seconds (30 seconds = ½ minute: 112 ÷ 2 = 56 beats).

At 112 bpm, there are 37⅓ beats in 20 seconds (20 seconds = ⅓ minute: 112 ÷ 3 = 37⅓ beats).

At 112 bpm, there are 18⅔ beats in 10 seconds (10 seconds = ⅙ of a minute: 112 ÷ 6 = 18⅔ beats).

By dividing the numbers in the $\frac{4}{4}$ or $\frac{3}{4}$ column by 2, you will get the number of measures in 30 seconds. By dividing the numbers in the $\frac{4}{4}$ or $\frac{3}{4}$ column by 4, you will get the number of measures in 15 seconds.

Figure 12.2 is a basic sequencer program chart that lets you document your work and see where things are for editing or chaining. For those of you who use sequencing software, the documentation potential is probably sufficient. If you use a dedicated sequencer, this chart may help you stay organized.

Modify the chart to suit your needs. One of the best ways to use it is to have a separate sheet for each part. For example, dedicate one sheet to the synth bass part, another to your pads or rhythmic comps, and so on. (Use a pencil.) The data will probably be moved, merged, and quantized any number of times. The sheet gives you an overview of the parts and the form.

Figure 12.1 is a generic drum machine programming sheet. It allows you to see everything that you have documented for a song or arrangement. This sheet helps keep all the important information about patterns, form, and so forth, organized. How many times have we programmed, reprogrammed, or edited drum patterns only to find that we forgot or lost some details? You can modify the sheet or use it as a model to construct a more personal version. (Hint: use a pencil; things change.)

Your Name or Logo

Project: _____ Artist: _____

Title: _____ Client: _____

Drum Machine (make and model): _____

Tempo: _____ bpm: _____ Type of Sync: _____

Track #: _____ Pattern Group(s): _____ _____

Program stored to: ❑Internal ❑Disk ❑Tape ❑Cartridge

File #: _____ (or Title): _____

Comments:

List Drum Voices Used: _____

❑Separate Outputs ❑Stereo Outputs ❑Mono Output

Pattern Number	How many times?	Description of Pattern

Figure 12.1

Your Name or Logo

Project: _____ Artist: _____

Title: _____ Client: _____

Sequencer (make and model): _____

Tempo: _____ bpm: _____ Type of Sync: _____

Program stored to: ❑Internal ❑Disk ❑Tape ❑Cartridge

File #: _____ (or Title): _____

Comments:

Track	MIDI Channel	Quantize/Step or Real Time	Description of Part

Figure 12.2

Arrangement Checklist

Below is a checklist of the important elements and considerations for any arrangements. These elements provide the balance, contrast, and unity needed to make an arrangement complete and sustain the listeners' interest. The music will hopefully be exciting and memorable. Many of these elements have already been discussed, but here they are again in one list.

1. The form is logical.

2. Melody and background contrast rhythmically.

3. Melody and background contrast in timbres.

4. Melody and background contrast in register.

5. Melody and background contrast in unison and voiced.

6. No single element is fighting for attention; the parts and sounds have clear priorities. Listeners can hear only two primary lines at once, in addition to the basic rhythm section or groove. Exceptions to this occur when you want to build excitement to a high level by layering in new elements.

7. Intro is written after you have worked out ideas for other sections of the arrangement.

8. Modulations are written to help singers make transitions comfortably, or the instant (surprise) modulations are well rehearsed. Use common tones, voice leading, and so forth.

9. Interludes are provided (when necessary) to let the listeners' ears digest the music and to provide contrast between sections.

10. Give the entire arrangement a rhythmic consistency test: Syncopations and downbeats of all parts lock in. Look for clashes that can distract the listener's attention. Unintentional conflicts between downbeats and syncopations can be caused by an oversight in the writing, inaccurate part copying, or player error.

11. Any doublings have a specific reason and are not haphazard or the result of not knowing what else to do.

12. Sounds are combined for a reason (see Number 11 above).

13. Spacing and register of voicings and parts follows the harmonic series. There should be no big gaps in voicings nor too many similar parts in the same register.

14. Voice leading is logical and consistent, making each melodic part coherent.

15. Balance between background and foreground: There are enough parts in each to provide depth and contrast in the overall arrangement.

16. Contrast between rhythmically active and sustained parts, with enough of each type of part.

17. Each part has its own well-defined sound and musical purpose.

18. All parts breathe.

19. Parts are accurately copied with complete instructions and musical markings.

20. Arrangement builds to a logical climax.

21. Sounds are in registers that are reasonable for the notes and parts they play.

22. Is the melody consistent within itself? (See the checklist in Chapter Two.)

23. Can you sing each part? Does it stand alone? Is it a complete musical statement?

24. The arrangement should have an overall feeling of simplicity, no matter how involved or complex a given part may be. You need predictability and surprise in all these elements:

    • *rhythm:* unexpected accents, silent beats, occasionally longer or shorter phrases surprise entrances.

    • *melody:* balance between expected and unexpected intervals, directions, rhythms.

    • *harmony:* balance between expected and surprise chords—modulations, deceptive cadences, reharmonization, substitutions.

    • *sounds:* balance between unusual and expected combinations and blends.

    • *style:* within any given style there is room for a certain amount of deviation from the expected clichés or idiomatic sounds and parts. Make an effort to expand or redefine elements of any style.

    • *form:* Within a given form, there is room for subtle changes or adjustments to keep the listeners' interest at a peak.

    • *dynamics:* There should be enough contrast in dynamics balanced between predictability and surprise.

25. Break any rule, but for a specific reason and goal. You will either have the technique or learn it as you go, (it will probably be a combination of both.) Whatever you do, do it with conviction. If it works, you will know immediately; and if it doesn't, it's not a failure. You are now one step closer to a solution.

CHAPTER THIRTEEN ✍
CONCLUSIONS

An arranger now needs more skills than ever. You have to be musically, technically, and psychologically skillful. In the course of any given project, you will encounter technical challenges and opportunities that didn't exist a few years ago. This makes the work that much more exciting, but it also puts a new, nonmusical pressure on you. How do you stay comfortable with the increasingly close relationship between timeless musical skills and rapidly evolving technology? At one extreme, you can put your head in the sand and choose not to deal with the problem. At the other extreme, you can pursue the latest advances in technology and temporarily abandon your music. Between these two extremes is a middle ground. If you are clear about the fact that music comes first and that technology provides exciting and useful tools to serve music, then you can go at a pace that is comfortable or not threatening to you. Take technology in stride, with a grain of salt. You can't master it all or all at once. What you can do is surround yourself with people knowledgeable in areas you lack. Build a support team of musical allies. Everyone has something to offer, including you. Do what you do best and associate with skillful people who want to help you or work with you. In this way you will assimilate the technological advances at a comfortable pace. Teamwork or collaboration is a great way to learn.

Beyond musical and technological skills, you need to master time management. There are only so many hours in the day, so make the best use of them. There are many good books and courses on time management that are worth investigating. *Time Management Made Easy* by Turla and Hawkins (Dutton) is one of the best. It is easy to lose your focus in the diversity of today's music world. Time management and goal setting will help keep you focused.

Most arranging is done under the pressure of deadlines. Sometimes this can inhibit creativity and experimentation when the pressure is too severe, but the pressure of a reasonable deadline can have a very positive effect. It will motivate you to choose a direction or approach, focus your ideas, set limitations and schedules, and work in a highly charged, disciplined way. Sometimes fear, if not too extreme, is a great motivator.

The Italian economist Vilfredo Pareto made an important discovery, which certainly applies to arranging. He found that 20 percent effort yields 80 percent results. This implies that your method of working must involve identifying priorities, setting goals, and monitoring your progress. Does the way you work produce the intended results? Also implied in Pareto's rule is that activity should not be confused with productivity. Lots of activity or paperwork doesn't necessarily mean anything of substance or value has been created. It's more important to work "smart" than "hard." This is similar to the practice-makes-perfect myth. Only perfect practice makes perfect, and if you are working hard, be sure it's also smart. All these suggestions are useless if you don't understand how to put them into practice. They must work for you in your pursuit of arranging skills.

Time management involves setting goals or targets and determining priorities. Set goals that are realistic and achievable. Build success into the process. If your goals are unrealistic, you will continually invalidate yourself and quit. This is a flexible process, not an exact science. Monitor your progress constantly and readjust your goals and targets to keep yourself focused and excited while accomplishing your goals.

Treat the techniques, exercises, and suggestions in each chapter as miniature goals. Give yourself small, doable projects with reasonable deadlines. Make a commitment to doing a project on time. As your technique grows, you will find yourself learning and accomplishing more in the same amount of time (maybe even less). This gets you used to working with deadlines and pressure.

You need goals to contain and focus your work. Working without a goal is like giving yourself permission to never get the job done: The task expands into the time allotted. If you tell yourself that you will get around to it, you either never will or you will panic at the last moment and cram for the deadline. We need reasonable goals, challenges, and pressure to perform. The idea is to accomplish the task, be proud of the work, and be rewarded for it.

Isolate one technique or suggestion and draw up a schedule, a specific goal, and a deadline. Put it in writing. Allow no distractions and specify a reward when you are finished. Schedule some relaxation time into the project. Don't lock yourself away working at a desperate, feverish pace, twenty-four hours a day until you drop from exhaustion or somehow manage to accomplish the goal.

This might be a realistic goal: "I want to analyze and transcribe drum parts from five R&B records this week. I'll work three hours a day for the next five days. I especially want to improve my understanding of kick-drum and bass-line relationships." Or, "I'm going to spend two hours a day, six days a week for a month, working on ear training (specifically on interval recognition and rhythmic dictation). I want to improve my ability to identify and notate parts of arrangements. I will work with a friend so we can take turns playing and writing out parts."

Don't be afraid to ask for help. Forget about any foolish pride. No one knows everything anyway. A know-it-all knows nothing at all. In fact, if you are not making mistakes (no matter what your level is), then you are probably not trying hard enough. Don't play it so safe that you are afraid to make the mistakes that will help you learn and grow.

Try to work at a time when your energy and concentration is fresh. This is your prime time. If that's not possible, clear your head out before you begin to work. If you can save twenty minutes per day by working more efficiently, times 5 days per week (100 minutes per week), times 50 work weeks per year, that will equal 5,000 minutes saved, or 83.3 hours in a year. That's a savings of over two work weeks of time (40 hours per week), just by working twenty minutes more efficiently per day. You can write a lot of music in approximately two weeks.

Find some allies—people who can actively help you and support your goals. Work together on a regular basis. Make it a priority to share ideas, problems, and possible solutions. Musicians are famous for "hangin' out." Often it is social, but it's just as much for the joy of sharing information and helping each other. Much of what you learn and master comes from working with people who have similar or complementary interests. There are really no secrets that can't be learned with patience and discipline.

There is a lot of truth in the belief that it's 90 percent perspiration and 10 percent inspiration. When you feel you are at a loss for ideas, you can always try some mechanical variations on a melody (for example, retrograde or inversion) to get the "juices flowing," or you can arbitrarily pick a few chords and turn a simple progression into a groove or basis for a song. You can also let your sequencer amuse you by running it through its paces on a few simple ideas.

One of the biggest problems we face is procrastination, which comes from fear or dislike of a certain task. This in turn causes anxiety. The net result is that you feel horrible, and nothing gets done. The way to conquer procrastination is to break a task into small, easy-to-handle parts and to work on individual aspects one at a time. Divide a task into a specific number of mini projects and set goals and time limits for their completion.

If you are not ready to deal with writing an entire arrangement end to end, that's fine. Don't run for cover. Work on different aspects of your musicianship in isolation. If the idea of developing an entire rhythm-section groove (never mind all the other parts) is overwhelming, pick one area and work with that. Maybe you will want to work on kick, snare, and hi-hat relationships for a while. Work slowly, deliberately, and patiently toward your declared goals.

If your purpose is to make a worthwhile contribution through your music and you are genuinely excited about it, the opportunities for exposure and money will present themselves. It also helps to develop your "people skills." This will play an important role in the quality and quantity of your work. An arranger works with many different personality types, often in close quarters and under pressure. Try to seek the common denominator in any group of people. If you actively pursue that approach rather than dig in in your heels on all your points, you will invariably get more ideas into the final arrangement.

There are opportunities to write arrangements in every town or city, such as local church groups, colleges, bar or club bands, home or commercial studios, theater groups, and community or civic organizations. Write as much and as often as you can for every kind of situation.

You may not get a paying job each time, but you may get creative freedom in place of it. Try to connect with a group that needs a lot of material on a regular basis. If you are not playing in the band, write for them as often as possible. Top-forty and show groups can provide you with an opportunity to dissect the current styles of arranging and to learn about technology at the same time. Approach as many people and situations as possible and offer your services. Get tapes of everything you do. The good ones will be useful demos of your work, and they will help generate more work. The tapes that don't turn out well are great learning experiences, too. Analyze them to see what went wrong. (Hopefully, this won't be that the players destroyed your well-written music.) Correct any of the writing problems, don't dismiss them. This way you will learn from mistakes instead of repeating them.

Make a list of your favorite groups; songwriters; arrangers; producers; and music from all styles, periods, and cultures. This collection of music will serve as a teacher and guide. When you approach an arrangement, ask yourself how one of these individuals would handle the situation. Let concepts from different styles or periods cross-pollinate into your writing. Allow some "hybrid vigor" to come into your music. Biologists say the strongest species are the hybrids, or mutts. Every piece of American music is the result of some intermarrying of musical styles or periods. Try to be flexible and eclectic in your approach to arranging. Deliberately try ideas that are not normal clichés. Try to incorporate them into an arrangement in an integral way, not in a gimmicky or superficial way. If the ideas don't fit, be prepared to let them go. Taking the "scenic route" always adds an interesting perspective to an arrangement. This will add new or unpredictable ideas to the final product.

It's impossible to develop as a musician if you don't really love your craft. It's easy to love it when the money rolls in, but your love and respect for music will carry you through the rough periods and help you survive and develop. In any important relationship, and music is no exception, you need some objectivity and a sense of humor. Sometimes the long hours and tentative rewards seem so absurd that you just have to laugh. Having a good sense of humor will make it bearable, and people will want to work with you.

When all the pieces finally fit together and the music sounds and feels great, it makes all the effort worthwhile. For many arrangers, the act of creating, not the performance, is most fulfilling. Nonetheless, in the end, most of us want to share our music.